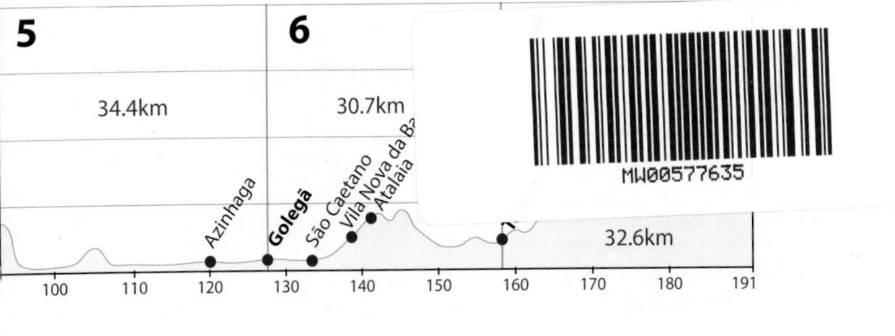

5
6
34.4km
30.7km
32.6km
Azinhaga
Golegã
São Caetano
Vila Nova da Ba
Atalaia
100
110
120
130
140
150
160
170
180
191

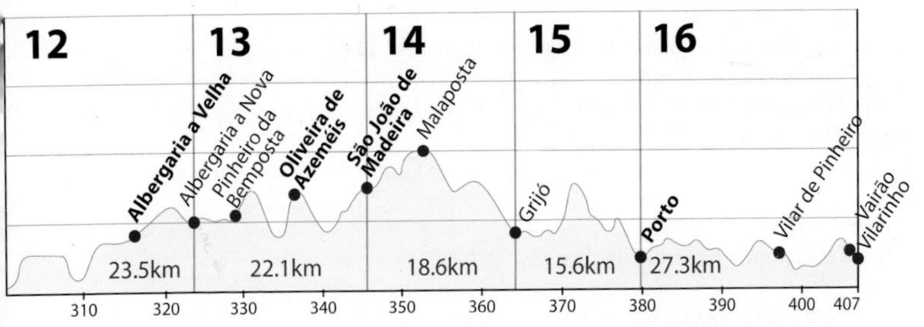

12
13
14
15
16
Albergaria a Velha
Albergaria a Nova
Pinheiro da Bemposta
Oliveira de Azeméis
São João de Madeira
Malaposta
Grijó
Porto
Vilar de Pinheiro
Vairão
Vilarinho
23.5km
22.1km
18.6km
15.6km
27.3km
310
320
330
340
350
360
370
380
390
400
407

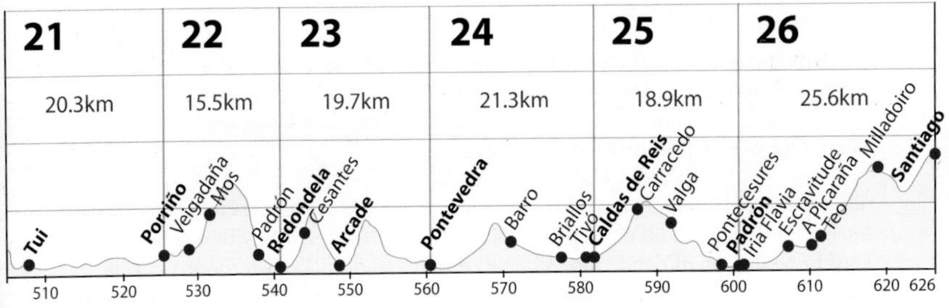

21
22
23
24
25
26
20.3km
15.5km
19.7km
21.3km
18.9km
25.6km
Tui
Porriño
Veigadaña
Mos
Padrón
Redondela
Cesantes
Arcade
Pontevedra
Barro
Briallos
Tivó
Caldas de Reis
Carracedo
Valga
Pontecesures
Padrón
Iria Flavia
Escravitude
A Picaraña
Teo
Milladoiro
Santiago
510
520
530
540
550
560
570
580
590
600
610
620
626

19a
20a
21a
22a
23a
28.4km
23.2km
16.5km
20.6km
15.5km
Carreço
Vila Praia de Âncora
Caminha
A Guarda
Oia
Viladesuso
Mougás
Baiona
A Ramallosa
Vigo
Redondela
90
100
110
120
130
140
150
160
170
180
186

have more transportation connections, food, lodging and other services.

Camino Portugués: Lisbon - Porto - Santiago, Central & Coastal Routes
Matthew Harms, Anna Dintaman, David Landis
1st edition, January 2018

Village to Village Press, LLC, Harrisonburg, VA, USA
www.villagetovillagepress.com

Photographs/Diagrams
All photographs and diagrams © Village to Village Press, LLC

Cover Photographs by Matthew Harms and David Landis
Front: Climb before As Mariñas on the Coastal Route
Back (left to right): Rio Douro near Porto, Santiago Cathedral, cobblestone near Pedreira

ISBN: 978-1-947474-02-4
Library of Congress Control Number: 2017916700

Cover and book design by David Landis

Disclaimer: *Every reasonable effort has been made to ensure that the information contained in this book is accurate. However, no guarantee is made regarding its accuracy or completeness. Reader assumes responsibility and liability for all actions in relation to using the provided information, including if actions result in injury, death, loss or damage of personal property or other complications.*

Contents

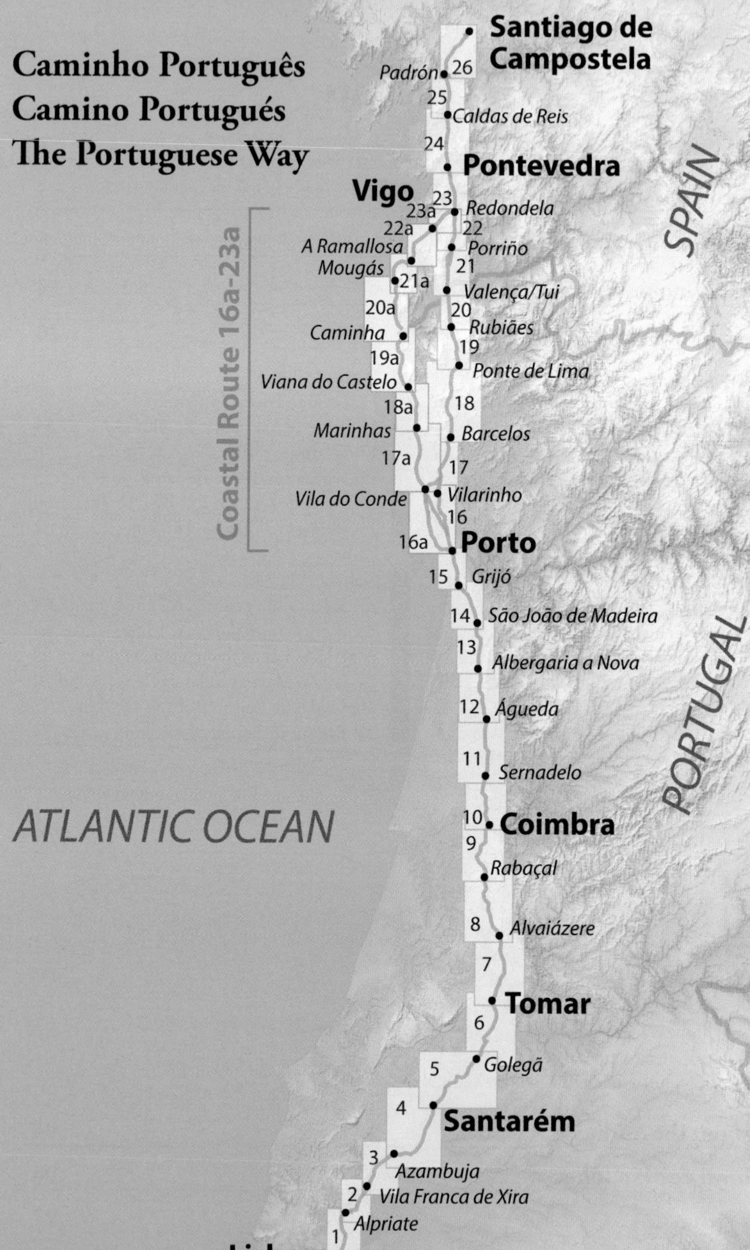
Caminho Português
Camino Portugués
The Portuguese Way
Santiago de Campostela
26
Padrón
25
Caldas de Reis
24
Pontevedra
SPAIN
Vigo
23
23a
Redondela
22a
22
A Ramallosa
Porriño
Mougás
21
21a
Valença/Tui
20a
20
Rubiães
Caminha
19
19a
Ponte de Lima
Viana do Castelo
18a
18
Marinhas
Barcelos
17a
17
Vila do Conde
Vilarinho
16
16a
Porto
Coastal Route 16a-23a
15
Grijó
14
São João de Madeira
13
Albergaria a Nova
12
Águeda
11
Sernadelo
PORTUGAL
ATLANTIC OCEAN
10
Coimbra
9
Rabaçal
8
Alvaiázere
7
Tomar
6
Golegã
5
4
Santarém
3
Azambuja
2
Vila Franca de Xira
Alpriate
1
Lisbon

The Portuguese Way

The ***Caminho Português*** is a pilgrimage route through Portugal into Spain, which culminates at the cathedral in Santiago de Compostela, where St. James is believed to be buried. Known in Spanish as the ***Camino Portugués*** and in English as the **Portuguese Way**, the route has become the second most popular in the Camino path network. When many people think of the "Camino" they are picturing the Camino Francés route, traversing from St-Jean-Pied-de-Port in France over the Pyrenees into Spain and due west to Santiago. In reality, there are many Caminos, echoing the ancient roads that pilgrims from all over Europe trod to visit the apostle's tomb. While the Francés route is by far the most popular, other routes are gaining in popularity.

While Saint James lore does exist along the Portuguese Way (especially around Padrón), the Portuguese Way is not as deeply steeped in Saint James history and stories as the Francés. Our Lady of Fátima (the Virgin Mary) is the primary patron saint of Portugal and and inspiration for modern-day pilgrimages. The Caminhos de Fátima (the Fátima Ways) are popular and used by pilgrims to visit the site of a 1917 appearance of the Virgin Mary. The Fátima routes are marked with blue arrows and lead to Fátima from all cardinal directions, often overlapping with the Camino.

The Portuguese Way has more walking on pavement and cobblestone and fewer (though still adequate) pilgrim-specific services than the Camino Francés. The route from Lisbon to Porto is the least developed as far as pilgrim services, since the majority of pilgrims start from Porto or later. Many of the accommodations listed as albergues in this book are actually hotels or pensions that offer a special rate for pilgrims in shared double or triple rooms. From Porto on, there are more dedicated pilgrim lodging options, though not as numerous or as frequent as on the Francés route. The route loosely follows the Roman Via Lusitana and was utilized for pilgrimage as early as the 12th century.

From Porto, the route presents several options which crisscross each other from time to time. The **Central Route** (stages 1-26) is the most traditional and popular option and goes north from Porto through the Portuguese interior to Galicia (stages 1-26). The **Coastal Route (**stages 16a-23a**)** stays closer to the coast, before rejoining the Central Route in Redondela, and has been gaining in popularity. Then the ***Senda Litoral*** (mapped for stage 16a) also follows the coast but stays on the coastline, sometimes along boardwalks and along the beach (stage 16a). The Senda Litoral is very scarcely marked and at times requires negotiating a rocky coastline with no clear path, but at times offers a pleasant walking option—we've tried to highlight the nicest sections in our maps of the Coastal Route.

St. James

"*[Jesus] saw two other brothers, James son of Zebedee and his brother John. They were in a boat with their father Zebedee, preparing their nets. Jesus called them, and immediately they left the boat and their father and followed him.*" Matthew 4:21-22

In the New Testament, St. James is referred to as a disciple of Jesus who left his trade as a fisherman to follow Jesus. The Bible tells us little about him, save that he requested to be seated at the right hand of Jesus in heaven and was present at many important events such as the Transfiguration and Jesus weeping in the Garden of Gethsemane. The last biblical mention of James is of his martyrdom in 44CE.

St. James became known as a patron saint of Portugal (and primary patron saint of Spain) thanks to tradition, oral history, legend and myth that tells of his ministry in the Iberian Peninsula. The story goes that James preached unsuccessfully in Iberia, attracting only seven disciples (Monte Santiaguiño along the Camino Portugués is traditionally the first place that James preached in Iberia). The Virgin Mary appeared to James with the pillar to which Jesus was tied to be whipped and instructed him to build a church in Zaragoza, Spain. Shortly after his encounter with Mary, James returned to Jerusalem and was martyred, and his body was transported to Spain on a stone ship without oars or sails, "carried by angels and the wind." The ship landed at Iria Flavia (present-day Padrón), and James' disciple met the ship there and transferred his body to be buried on a nearby hill.

The body of St. James was forgotten until 813CE, when a Christian hermit named Pelayo saw a light that led him to the grave. The bishop authenticated these relics, and King Alfonso II built a chapel to the saint. The current cathedral was begun in the year 1075 and completed in the 1120s. The event that catapulted this modest shrine to a major pilgrimage site was the mythical Battle of Clavijo in 852, when St. James was said to have appeared to assist the Christian army against Muslim invaders. This story mirrors Muslim legends about Muhammad appearing in battle to assist the Muslim forces. This image of St. James was a convenient motif to draw Christian support to the frontier of Christian-Muslim battle and to bolster interest and financial investment in maintaining Christian domination of Iberia.

Pilgrimage to Santiago reached its zenith in the 11th-12th centuries, with reports of 1,000 pilgrims a day arriving to the cathedral. There was high interest in relics, and infrastructure for pilgrims increased, including the establishment of the Spanish Military Order of Santiago to protect pilgrims. Many churches and monasteries provided lodging for pilgrims. Santiago de Compostela became one of the three main Christian pilgrimage sites, along with Rome and Jerusalem.

Medieval Pilgrimage

For most medieval pilgrims, the path to Santiago entailed a grueling journey of six months to one year. As today, pilgrims came with diverse purposes and motivations. A major motivation was *orandi causa*—in order to pray, to seek forgiveness, to fulfill a vow, or to petition St. James for a certain blessing, such as healing. The pilgrimage was sometimes "prescribed" by a priest or religious official as penance for a crime committed. No official records can confirm that medieval pilgrims set out on the road out of a thirst for adventure, but in the provincial lives of many peasants who rarely left their own tiny hamlets and villages, such a pilgrimage must surely have been attractive as one adventurous journey that could be justified with pious purposes.

Pilgrims came from all strata of society, from royalty and wealthy landowners by horse and carriage, to middle class artisans and workers on horseback, to peasants, paupers and beggars on foot. Without the convenience of credit and ATM cards, medieval pilgrims carried their coins sewn into the lining of their cloaks and were often easy prey for thieves and dishonest money changers.

Medieval pilgrims had a certain style of dress that can still be noted in depictions of St. James as a pilgrim. Pilgrims wore short cloaks so as not to interfere with walking but to still provide warmth. A wide-brimmed hat protected from both sun and rain. Beside these practical clothing items, pilgrims carried several symbolic items. One was the ***bordón***, a wooden staff that symbolized of the wood of the cross of Christ. Pilgrims carried the ***escarcela***, a leather bag that was flat and narrower at the top than the bottom. The bag reminded pilgrims to carry little and rely on God's provision. There was no closure on the bag, to remind pilgrims to give and receive freely.

The final symbolic item was the **scallop shell**, which is common along the Galician coast. The *Codex Calixtinus* describes the shell as representing the fingers of an open hand, symbolizing the good deeds expected of a pilgrim. Another interpretation is that the lines of the shell, which converge at a single point, represent the pilgrimage roads convening in Santiago. While medieval pilgrims only bore the symbol of the shell upon their return journey, today many pilgrims wear a shell on their way to Santiago. Those who died along the path were buried with their shell.

Many pilgrims died, leaving thousands of graves along the Camino. Pilgrimage was fraught with many dangers, including finding drinkable water, crossing rivers, exorbitant tolls at mountain passes, lice and fleas, bandits, thieves and murderers. Therefore, pilgrims traveled in groups mainly made up of men. Most hospices provided large straw mattresses that were shared by dozens of people. These hardships were viewed as an integral part of the pilgrim experience, identifying with the *Via Dolorosa* or 'way of suffering' undertaken by Jesus on his way to the cross.

The Camino Experience

The Camino de Santiago is a network of historical pilgrim routes throughout Europe that lead to Santiago de Compostela in Spain, the traditional burial place of Saint James. The experience is quite unique from most long-distance walking routes around the world. Rather than a remote wilderness trek, the Camino weaves through villages, towns and even large cities. Walkers need not carry a heavy pack since frequent hostels and restaurants mean you can forego a tent, sleeping bag, and food resupply. The more popular Camino routes, such as the Francés and Portugués, are well-trodden enough that you can be practically guaranteed walking companions in almost any season other than winter.

Many walkers undertake the Appalachian, Pacific Crest Trail or similar for wilderness and solitude, neither of which are primary experiences on the Camino. The Camino offers camaraderie, encounters with culture and history, and, for many, a spiritual experience. Since the Camino routes were historically used for religious pilgrimage, anyone walking the Camino is generally considered a pilgrim, even if you are walking more for sport than spirituality.

This information will get you started, and more extensive details are online.

Pilgrim Practicalities

The ***Credencial*** or "**pilgrim passport**" is a document carried by Camino walkers that allows access to pilgrim lodging and also bestows free or reduced entry to some museums and cathedrals. Collect stamps (*carimbos* in Portuguese, *sellos* in Spanish) at accommodations and other landmarks, which serve as proof of completing the pilgrimage to receive a *Compostela*.

The ***Compostela*** is a document of completion awarded to those who walk at least the last 100km to Santiago or complete the last 200km by bicycle or on horseback. Present your completed credencial at the pilgrim office in Santiago in order to get your Compostela, written in Latin and personalized with your name and date of completion. Be sure to collect at least two stamps per day for the last 100km. Cardboard tubes are available for carrying your Compostela back home safely.

When to Go & Trip Length

While the Camino can be walked in any season, spring and autumn are generally considered the best times of year to have cooler weather and avoid summer crowds.

Spring - Pleasant temperatures, flowers in bloom, most services open, more likely than summer or fall to encounter rain
Summer - Most popular and crowded, weather can be very hot, all services open
Autumn - Pleasant temperatures, most services open
Winter - Cold and rainy with potential for snow, many services closed, still possible if adequately prepared

How much time do I need? This full itinerary from Lisbon to Santiago takes about four weeks, and is best experienced with time built in for rest days and shorter days when necessary. We have split up the journey to Santiago into 26-27 daily stages, with an average daily distance of 24km (15mi). Feel free to deviate from this pace, staying at intermediary accommodations, which are noted on maps and in the text. If you have less time, consider starting in Porto (246km) or Tui (118km).

Visas and Entry

Portugal and Spain are both among the 26 Schengen states of the European Union (EU) that have no internal borders. Citizens of the USA, Canada, Australia, New Zealand and some South American countries are issued a free visa upon arrival with valid passport, limited to 90 days within a 180-day period. Most African, Asian, Middle Eastern and some South American nationalities must apply for an advance visa. Check EU regulations to see if your nationality requires an advance visa.

Collecting stamps in the credencial

Sleeping

One of the unique features of the Camino routes is the network of affordable pilgrim lodging known as ***abrigos*** in Portuguese, but more commonly called by the Spanish term ***albergues.*** Albergues are simple **dormitory accommodations** intended for non-motorized pilgrims (traveling on foot, by bicycle or on horse). They are generally operated by the local municipality, parish, pilgrim confraternity, or a private owner. Many operate on a first-come first-serve basis, though most private albergues accept reservations. Lower cost albergues often fill up quite early in the day during popular seasons.

Costs typically range between €5-15 per person, with some albergues operating on a donation basis (*donativo*). Amenities range from very basic to all the "bells and whistles" like wifi, washer, dryer, guest kitchen, etc. Amenities are shown in the text through symbols (p. 97). Accommodations with their own website have a (links listed at **caminoguidebook.com**). Unless otherwise noted, assume that all albergues offer a mattress, pillow, bathroom with shower, and a place to handwash clothing. It's expected that you will bring a sleeping bag or sleep sack, and albergues often do not change bed sheets every day. The person in charge of an albergue is called a *hospitalero* (male) or *hospitalera* (female), and is often a volunteer.

In areas with fewer dedicated pilgrim services, such as the path between Lisbon and Porto, **hotels** and **pensions** often offer special pilgrim prices. **Fire stations** (***bombeiros voluntários***) also sometimes provide basic lodging, though this is becoming less common as more albergues open. We do list stations that are known to offer this, but it's best to consider them as backup or overflow to more formal accommodations. Portugal offers a wide range of accommodations types, from simple rooms with shared bathrooms in family-run pensions to opulent hotels.

Lodging amenities are shown in the text through symbols (legend inside back cover). A **Hostel/Albergue** prices refer to a dormitory bed. If a hostel also has A H **private rooms**, the prices indicate dorm bed/single room/double room prices (€10/30/50). For H **hotels**, we list the single (if available)/double prices per room. Most albergues are open from around April 1 to November 1, with some staying

Bed Bugs, or *Cimex lectularius,* a blood-sucking parasitic insect, are on the rise around the world and have been a problem in accommodations along the Camino in recent years. While bed bugs do not carry any known diseases, bites can be very uncomfortable and cause painful rashes for some people, and the insects are very difficult to get rid of once infested. Some ways to avoid bed bugs include pretreating your sleeping bag and backpack with permethrin or other insect repellent and checking that any albergue you stay in has been fumigated recently.

open for winter or year round. While there are a few formal ▲ **campgrounds** on the route, carrying a tent is uncommon as "wild/free camping" is not generally permitted in Portugal and Spain, and reasonably priced lodging is available each night.

Eating

Cafes and restaurants are readily available most days. Larger towns and cities have grocery stores if you wish to carry a packed lunch or snacks, and there is usually no need to carry more than that. Cafes in Portugal typically offer meat and cheese sandwiches (*sanduíche fiambre e queijo*) and pastries like *pastel de nata* (egg custard tart) for breakfast, lunch or a snack break. *Galão* (espresso with foamed milk) is the breakfast beverage of choice.

In Spain, try a hearty wedge of egg and potato *tortilla* and Galician specialties like boiled octopus (*Pulpo a la Feira*), and *cafe con leche* for your caffeine needs. Dinner often includes a set menu (starter, main dish, wine, bread and dessert for around €8-12) or plate of the day offering a combination of several dishes. On maps, we do not distinguish between bars/cafés and restaurants, as both normally offer drinks and food. Some lodging has a guest kitchen where you could cook your own meal. With special dietary considerations, such as gluten free, vegetarian or vegan, it may be challenging to find food that fits your needs in restaurants, espeically since meat and animal products are staples of Portuguese and Spanish cuisine. Grocery stores in cities typically have a wide variety of foods including gluten free products, so plan ahead and carry some extra supplies.

Breakfast spread on the Camino

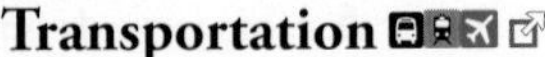

Transportation

Lisbon and Porto both have **airports** accessible from major cities in Europe by budget flight (Madrid, Barcelona, Paris, London among others). **Train** (*Comboios de Portugal*: cp.pt) and **bus** (*Renex*: renex.pt) connections also exist. For best train prices, book five or more days ahead. Towns and cities with daily bus and train access are labeled with respective symbols in stage chapters. Taxis are also an option, as well as car rental from major population centers. Hitchhikers are rarely picked up and should assume all known risks.

Money, Costs and Budgeting

The unit of **currency** in Portugal and Spain is the euro, made up of 100 euro cents. The best way to obtain euros is to use ATM/cash machines, available in cities and many towns marked in text with symbol. Pilgrim hostels and small town amenities usually work on a cash basis, but some hotels, restaurants, stores accept credit cards. **Daily costs** for many pilgrims are simply lodging, food/drink and sometimes incidentals like first aid supplies, laundromat or luggage transfer. An average daily budget probably falls in the €30-50 range, depending on your frugality, though it may be possible to spend a bit less and definitely to spend a lot more, particularly if you prefer hotels to hostels. Currency: US $1 ≈ EU €0.86, EU €1 ≈ US $1.16, EU €1 ≈ UK £0.88

Phones and Internet

For phone coverage, you have the options of enabling international roaming on your home mobile phone plan or purchasing a **Portuguese SIM card** (which requires an unlocked GSM phone). **International roaming** on many US and Canada based plans is often quite expensive, but can be a good solution if only used in case of emergency. T-Mobile has free international data and text on some of their US plans. European plans tend to have inexpensive roaming within Europe. Calling and messaging apps like WhatsApp, Viber or Skype can be used when you have a wifi connection if you choose not to have cellular data coverage.

Country codes and dialing internationally

- To call Portugal (+351) from the USA, landline: 011 - 351 - 2 - XXXX-XXXX
- To call Portugal (+351) from the USA, mobile: 011 - 351 - 9 - XXXX-XXXX
- To call Spain (+34) from the USA: 011 - 34 - XXX-XXXX
- To call the USA and Canada (+1) from abroad: 00 - 1 - XXX-XXX-XXXX

Wifi (pronounced "wee-fee") is increasingly available along the route; many accommodations and cafés offer free (if slow) access. Some lodgings still have **desktop computers** for guest use while larger cities often have internet cafés, though they are both becoming more rare with the prevalence of handheld devices.

Luggage Transfer and Tours

Transfer services cost **€5-10 per day** to pick up luggage at one accommodations and deliver it to the next. Weight (<15kg) and distance (<30km) restrictions often apply. Usually service must be facilitated with reservation-based private albergues or hotels, not municipal or parochial albergues. Remember to still carry water, snacks and a medical kit in a daypack during your walk. Tui Trans operates from Porto to Santiago. There is no formal service between Lisbon and Porto, but your lodging may be able to make arrangements with a private taxi.

Medical Care

Portugal and Spain have good medical care that is free for citizens and members of countries with reciprocal agreements. Citizens of Great Britain, Ireland and the EU need a European Health Insurance Certificate (EHIC). US, Canadian and other non-EU citizens are recommended to have private health and travel insurance. Carry an emergency contact card with known allergies, pertinent medical history and information that is helpful to medical staff if you are unable to communicate. In emergencies, dial ✆112 to reach emergency services. Pharmacies are well-stocked and readily available in cities and larger towns.

Safety Issues

Portugal and Spain have very low crime rates, and violent crime is extremely rare. However, it is always good to remain aware of your surroundings, not leave valuables unattended, and report any incidents to the police as soon as possible by dialing ✆112. As the route sometimes follows paved roads with fast **traffic**, a reflective vest and bright clothing are recommended. Be extremely careful when crossing roads. Always walk on the left side of the road opposite traffic and remain alert. Try to avoid walking near or after dark. Aggressive **dogs** are not common but may be encountered. Carrying a walking stick can enhance confidence when encountering animals. All dogs in Portugal and Spain are required to be vaccinated against rabies.

Associação de Peregrinos Via Lusitana

The Portuguese pilgrim association, Via Lusitana, is very active in promoting and improving the Caminho Português, including updating waymarks and signage. The association also operates a 24-hr emergency hotline for pilgrims: ✆915595213 as well as a useful website (though currently only in available in Portuguese) **vialusitana.org**.

Additional planning information is available online at **caminoguidebook.com** and **caminocyclist.com**.

CAMINO CYCLIST

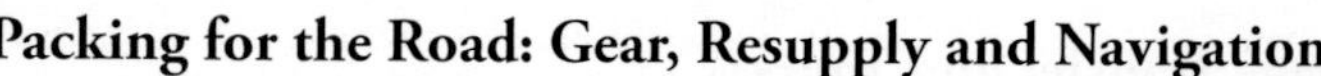

Packing for the Road: Gear, Resupply and Navigation

He who would travel happily must travel light. -Antoine de Saint-Exupéry

A light load makes for a happy pilgrim, and weight should be a primary concern in packing. A popular guideline is to pack no more than 10% of your body weight. Resist the temptation to pack many extras "just in case." Shops are readily available in Portugal and Spain and most anything lacking can be purchased along the way.

Backpacks: A 30-40L (1800-2500in^3) pack is sufficient for warm weather (40-60L for winter). Measure your torso length and choose a pack of the proper size, preferably being fitted at a knowledgeable outdoor retail store. Aim for a pack that weighs less than 1.4kg (3lbs) when empty.

Footwear: Light boots or sturdy trail runners with a stiff or semi-rigid sole offer protection for your feet and ankles against the often hard-surfaced, rocky and uneven path (trail surfaces, p. 18). Get fitted for footwear in the afternoon or evening after feet have expanded during the day. Bring some kind of lightweight footwear to wear in the evenings, such as flip-flops or foam sandals. ⚠ Be sure to thoroughly break in your footwear before beginning the Camino with practice hikes wearing your loaded pack. Invest in wool socks (not cotton), which wick moisture away from your skin, dry quickly, insulate when wet and manage odor better. If you're prone to blisters, experiment with liner socks (wool or polypropylene) to create an extra rubbing layer other than your skin.

Sleeping Bags: Most pilgrims prefer a lightweight, mummy-style, 1-season summer sleeping bag (rated $^+$40+°F/$^+$5+°C) for the summer season. Some opt for only a sleeping bag liner in the heat of summer. For winter and the cool edges of fall and spring, it's a good idea to have a 3-season sleeping bag (rated $^+$15-$^+$35°F/$^-$10-0°C. Buy the lightest bag you can afford within your desired temperature range.

Clothing: Consider hiking clothes as layers, with inner layers for moisture management, middle for insulation and outer for weather protection. The general rule for outdoor clothing is to avoid cotton as it does not retain insulating properties when wet and dries slowly. Synthetic materials (polyester, nylon, spandex) and wool (especially merino) are preferred, especially in cold and wet weather. In warm seasons, choose lightweight breathable clothes that provide sun protection.

Be prepared for the sun with a wide-brimmed **hat** and **sunglasses,** and use **sunscreen** regularly. Bring a **lightweight rain jacket** with a waterproof breathable membrane, or use a poncho that can also cover your backpack. Bring a waterproof pack cover or line your pack with plastic garbage bags to keep your gear dry. Pack electronics in zippered plastic bags or dry bags to protect against moisture.

Hypothermia is possible in wet, cool weather, so be prepared with a dry set of clothes (socks included) for after a rainy day and bring one insulating layer, such as a warm fleece or down sweater.

Water and refills: While water is readily available most days of the Camino, it is important to carry sufficient amounts. Always carry at least one liter, and refill often; carry more than two liters on hot days or in more remote areas. Reliable water refill sites are marked on stage maps (🚰). Tap water in Portugal and Spain is treated and drinkable (potable). Most historic springs are marked as undrinkable (*no potable*) because they have not been treated or tested. Bottled water is widely available, but less environmentally-friendly than refillable bottles.

Dehydration and heat-related illness: Dehydration can lead to fatigue, headaches, heat exhaustion and heat stroke (a dangerous and life-threatening condition). Be sure to eat foods that help to replenish electrolytes and consider an electrolyte drink, such as Aquarius™, on hot days. If you become dehydrated and overheated and are unable to cool down, take a break in a cool, shady place, rehydrate with electrolytes and cool with a wet cloth or fanning until you feel better.

Fitness and Training: The Camino is not a technically challenging hike, but the journey's length and hard surfaces day after day takes a toll on the body. Taking the time to practice before beginning the pilgrimage will greatly reduce possible injuries. Training walks will help you get used to your gear, the weight on your feet and shoulders and any other potential issues you might be able to prevent. It's wise to get used to full-day walks, taking 2-3 shorter walks per week and one full-day walk weekly with your loaded backpack. Check with your doctor if you have concerns about your health or fitness level, and start out slow and gradual.

Blister Prevention: The most common injury can cause an end to your trip.

- At home: choose properly fitting footwear. Try on many options before buying (foot should not move or slip when walking on various terrain types and grades). Use wool socks and liners. Break in footwear by taking hikes with a loaded pack prior to beginning the Camino.
- On the trail: keep feet cool and dry, take off shoes and socks for breaks, wash feet and socks daily, use liner socks.

Packing List

Hiking Gear Essentials

- ☐ **Backpack** (30-40L)
- ☐ **Sleeping bag or bag liner**, lightweight
- ☐ **Navigation**: guidebook, GPS (optional)
- ☐ **Headlamp** or flashlight/torch
- ☐ **Sun protection**: hat, sunglasses, sunscreen and lip balm
- ☐ **Towel**, lightweight travel type
- ☐ **Water bottles** and/or **hydration system** (2L)
- ☐ **Waterproof pack cover/poncho**
- ☐ **Pocket/utility knife** (checked luggage)
- ☐ **Lighter** or **matches** (buy locally)
- ☐ **Toiletries** (list opposite)
- ☐ **Personal items** (list opposite)
- ☐ **First aid kit** (list opposite)

Take the time to visit a quality outdoor gear shop to get fitted for a backpack that is comfortable and footwear that fits properly.

Footwear & Clothing

- ☐ **Footwear** (boots or trail runners)
- ☐ **Sandals** or flip-flops
- ☐ **Hiking socks** (3 pairs wool)
- ☐ **Sock liners** (1-2 pairs wicking)
- ☐ **Pants** (1-2 pairs quick-drying, zip-offs, or shorts)
- ☐ **Short-sleeved shirts**, tank tops (1-2)
- ☐ **Long-sleeved shirts** (1-2)
- ☐ **Light fleece** or jacket
- ☐ **Waterproof jacket** or poncho
- ☐ **Underwear** (3 pairs)
- ☐ **Sports bras** (2)
- ☐ **Bandana** or Buff
- ☐ **Swimsuit** (optional)
- ☐ **Warm hat***
- ☐ **Insulating jacket***
- ☐ **Long underwear** top/bottom*

**only necessary in cold seasons*

Additional Gear (Optional)

- ☐ **Hiking poles**: Used correctly, poles can take up to 25% pressure off of your leg joints. Poles are great for stability, especially going up and down hills, and serve double-duty as a means to chase away dogs. Worthwhile for anyone with joint issues. Inexpensive poles can be purchased in on route.
- ☐ **Sleeping mat**: A lightweight foam pad can come in handy for sitting on and for sleeping if albergues are full or have limited beds. You can often find left behind mats for free along the Camino.
- ☐ **Pillowcase**: Most albergues have pillows but do not change the pillowcases regularly, a spare T-shirt can also be stretched over the pillow as a makeshift case.
- ☐ **Stuff sacks** or cloth bags with drawstrings don't weigh much and keep you organized
- ☐ **Reusable nylon grocery bag**: Comes in handy as a laundry bag, purse and grocery bag
- ☐ **Clothespins** or safety pins for hanging laundry.
- ☐ **Travel cooking pot and utensils**: Many of the albergues in Galicia have kitchens, but no kitchen equipment whatsoever. If you are intent on cooking your own dinners, you may wish to bring a lightweight cooking pot, or purchase one when you arrive in Galicia.
- ☐ **Camping gear:** Lightweight tent (TarpTent) or bivy sack, camping stove, a pot and utensils, and extra water carrying capacity. (See Camping p. ___).

***For recommendations on specific brands and models, visit caminoguidebook.com.**

***Decathlon** is a chain of outdoor gear retailers throughout Portugal and Spain with stores in Lisbon, Santarém, Coimbra, Porto, Vigo and Santiago de Compostela, as well as Madrid and Barcelona.

Toiletries

Don't pack too much. Bring small refillable travel bottles of shampoo and conditioner <100mL/4oz. Refill from items left behind (ask at the albergues) or buy your own refill and share.

- ☐ **Shampoo/conditioner** (100mL/4oz bottles)
- ☐ **Toothbrush** and **toothpaste** (travel sized)
- ☐ **Soap**, biodegradable bar or liquid, such as Dr. Bronner's™
- ☐ **Laundry detergent** (powder works well and weighs less) or 100mL/4 oz. bottle or solid bar
- ☐ **Toilet paper** or tissues (albergues frequently run out)
- ☐ **Deodorant** (optional, you will stink with or without it!)
- ☐ **Hand sanitizer** (optional)
- ☐ **Contact solution** (if necessary), replace at pharmacies

First Aid/Medical Kit

Supplies are available in pharmacies along the route and most albergues have a basic medical kit. It's always best to be prepared with at least a few day's worth of each supply. Keep it light!

- ☐ Any **prescription medicine** you need
- ☐ Variety of **Band-Aids®/plasters, sterile gauze pads**
- ☐ Antiseptic towelettes or **wound disinfectant**
- ☐ **Antibiotic ointment**
- ☐ **Medical tape**
- ☐ **Elastic bandage** (such as ACE™)
- ☐ **Pain reliever/fever reducer** (such as acetaminophen or ibuprofen)
- ☐ **Antihistamine** (such as Benadryl®)
- ☐ **Anti-diarrheal** medicine: loperamide hydrochloride (Imodium®)
- ☐ **Blister treatment** (such as Moleskin or Compeed®)
- ☐ **Safety pins**
- ☐ **Baby powder** (helps with chafing)
- ☐ Small **scissors** and **tweezers**

Personal Items (Optional)

- ☐ **Travel wallet**: with passport/ID, health insurance card, pilgrim passport, money, credit cards, ATM card, etc. Stash an extra ATM card or wad of cash somewhere separate from your wallet.
- ☐ **Earplugs**: high quality noise-canceling earplugs are essential for a good night's sleep.
- ☐ **Mobile phone** and **charger** (see Phones and Internet p. ___)
- ☐ **Camera, charger, memory cards**, compact USB flash drive for backup
- ☐ **Journal with pen/pencil**: highly recommended for remembering the details of each day, reflecting more fully on the experience and recording contact info of new friends.
- ☐ **Tablet or e-reader:** useful for checking email and for pleasure reading without carrying heavy books. Photos of family and home are good conversation starters.
- ☐ **Book** for pleasure reading (just bring one and trade when you're done)
- ☐ **Plug/currency converter** for any electrical appliances (European plugs run on 220V with two round prongs. Most electronics run on 110-220V, labeled on device, requiring only a plug converter and not a currency converter.)
- ☐ **Zippered plastic bags or waterproof stuff sacks** for keeping electronics and other valuables dry and organized.
- ☐ **Pilgrim's shell**

Blister Treatment

- Take a break, remove socks to let feet cool and dry out. Check for hot spots and address by applying moleskin, Compeed®, or duct tape to create an additional rubbing surface to protect the hot spot.
- If a blister forms, use a sterilized needle to puncture its edge near the skin and drain using sterile materials. Air dry and re-dress blister with sterile bandages.
- If the blister or surrounding area becomes infected over the course of several days (increasing red appearance, tenderness, pus, red streaks), see a doctor.

For **dry and cracked feet**, consider wearing socks all the time to keep moisture in for cracks to heal. In severely painful cracks, a tiny bit of super glue can be helpful to hold the crack together, but make sure to clean the area thoroughly with soap, water and antiseptic.

Impact-related injuries are common with the large amount of paved surfaces on the Camino. If your feet and joints are taking a pounding, consider reducing your daily distance, walking on the softer shoulder near the paved path or adding walking poles and/or thicker socks.

The Trail: The paths that make up the Camino de Santiago covered in this book span over 800km (500 miles) and vary greatly in trail surface, grade, landscapes, ecosystem and climate. Proportionately, the Camino has more paved surfaces than many hikers expect including many sections of cobblestone, contributing to stress on feet and joints. P Paved/ U Unpaved designations in this book refer to most obvious walking surface. There may be unpaved shoulders or footpaths along paved roads.

Route Finding, Trail Markings, Maps and GPS → The Camino Portugués is generally well-marked, with a few sections where marks are more scarce and faded. The most common waymarks are painted yellow arrows →, though a variety of other markings exist in different regions that incorporate yellow arrows or scallops shells into posts or signs. Blue arrow waymarks indicate the Fátima pilgrimage, which follows the Camino route from Lisbon to Santarém (where the routes diverge) but lead in the opposite direction after Alvaiázere.

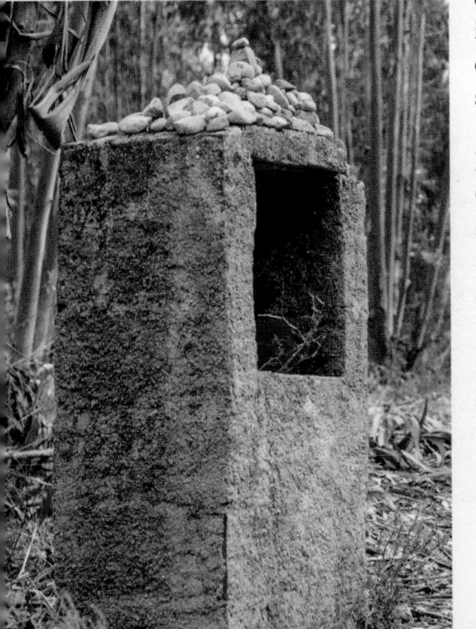

The path is well marked with yellow arrows.

The most difficult sections to navigate are through large cities, where routes are often poorly marked and Camino markers compete with other signs. For this reason, we've included a number of detailed city maps throughout this book, though note that the maps are representative and not exhaustive, without every street name. **GPS files are on our website, as well as tips on smart phone navigation.**

Daily Stages and Regional Sections: This book organizes the Camino Portugués into 26-27 daily stages averaging about 24km (15 miles) per day. The page spreads introducing each stage include a stage map, elevation profile, total distance, paved/unpaved (P/U) percentages, difficulty level (see below), time estimate and a list of towns with pilgrim hostels or albergues.

Stages begin and end at the main or largest albergue in the beginning and ending locality whenever possible. For mid-stage towns and points of interest without albergues, measurements are taken from the town center or main church, whichever is closest to the marked route or prominent. Cumulative stage distances are noted on the stage maps and correspond to distances listed in stage chapter text and town listings. Distances for off-route accommodations or points of interest are indicated with a plus symbol (example: +1.3km). Towns list resources available, all the albergues and a selection of private accommodations in varying price ranges.

Distances are measured in kilometers and meters. Estimated **walking time** for each stage assumes a pace of 3-4 km/hr (1.8-2.5 mph) with difficulty in terrain and elevation change considered. Factor extra time for breaks and exploration. Each day's stage route is assigned a **difficulty level** from 1-3. These ratings consider an "average" walker, who is reasonably fit but not necessarily athletic.

Length:
1m = 1yd or 3ft
100m ≈ 100yd
1km = 0.62 miles
10km = 6.2 miles
1.6km = 1 mile

Easy: Slight elevation change, sturdy footing, water easily accessible
Moderate: Some elevation change, moderately challenging terrain
Challenging: Significant elevation change, possibly rocky or narrow path with less stable footing, water sources may be scarce

This **map guidebook** is designed to be lightweight and minimalist. It provides detailed stage and city maps, pilgrim lodging as well as select hotels, listing of amenities in relevant towns and cities, and basic preparation, background information, and tips when helpful. This book does not include comprehensive route descriptions, extensive historical background information, nor all hotel listings.

Visit **caminoguidebook.com** for expanded planning information.

1 LISBON TO ALPRIATE

22.0km (13.7mi), 5.5-7 Hours, Difficulty:
P 61%, 13.4km, U 39%, 8.7km

In Lisbon, the ***credencial*** (pilgrim passport) and ***carimbo*** (stamp) are available in the Basílica dos Mártires (9am-5pm) and Sé Cathedral (10am-5pm).

See pages 22-23 for city map and tips for navigating out of Lisbon. The albergue in Alpriate is well worth a visit and makes for a soft landing on this first walking day. An ambitious walker can combine the first three days into two by walking Lisbon to Verdelha de Baixo (32.1km - 1.4km off-route; no albergue but inexpensive pensions), then Verdelha de Baixo to Azambuja (31.4km). If in doubt, start off slow and be careful not to overextend yourself. Some pilgrims skip the first 8km of urban walking by starting from the Oriente train station or Pousada de Juventude in Moscavide.

0.0 Lisbon A H

See city map and accommodations list on p. 22-23.

8.4 Parque das Nações H

H **Olissippo Oriente** (€75+): , República 15, 213182790, +200m
H **TRYP Oriente** (€80+): , D. João II, 218930000, +600m
H **Ibis** (€60+): , Mar Vermelho, 210730470, +600m
H **VIP Executive Arts** (€70/80): , D. João II 47, 210020400, +900m

9.8 Moscavide A H

A H **Pousada de Juventude** (72, €15-17/-/34-44): , Moscavide, Lt 47-101, 218920890, 925665076, +700m

22.0 Alpriate A

No supermarket in Alpriate, but there are a few cafés that also sell some basic food items.

A **Alpriate** (assoc, 12, €8): , 915595213, Mar-Oct, Run by the Vía Lusitana association and staffed by volunteers.

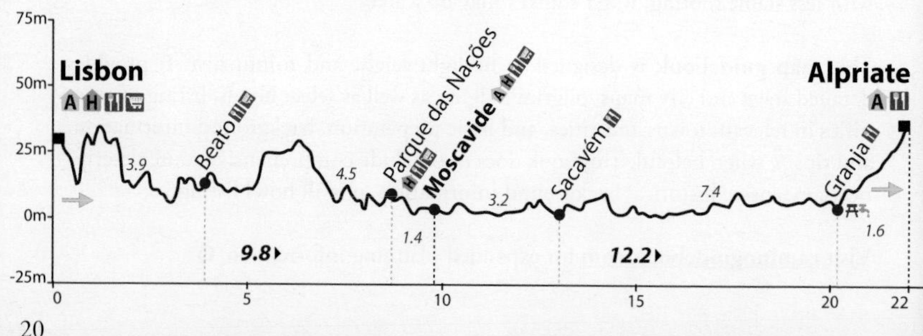

N-115
N-10
A-9
Granja
22.0
Alpriate
A
Bombeiros, see stage 2
20.4
Póvoa de Santa Iria
N-115
N-115-5
From Alpriate, 8.7km to turn-off to Verdelha de Baixo
Santa Iria
Santa Iria de Azoia
A-8
E-9
São João da Talha
A-30
Frielas
Rio Trancão
Santa António dos Cavaleiros
Unhos
N-10
N-250
Bobadela
Bobadela
Camarate
13.0
A-36
A-30
11.7
Roulote
Sacavém
Prior Velho
N-10
Skate Park
IP-7
A-12
Rio Tejo
E-9
Moscavide
9.8
A H
Pousada de Juventude, +700m
VIP Arts
9.2
Torre de Vasco da Gama
Ibis
H
Cable Car
Lisbon Airport
TRYP Oriente
8.4
Parque das Nações
Oriente
A-12
Olissippo
H
Oceanarium
Hospital
Underpass
6.5
Cross Av. Infante Dom Henrique and angle slightly L onto cobblestone side street: R. Vale Formoso
5.3
Beato
3.9
Teatro Ibérico
3.0
N
Lisbon
A H
Santa Apolónia
Sé Cathedral
Museo do Fado
0.0
2 km
0
1
2

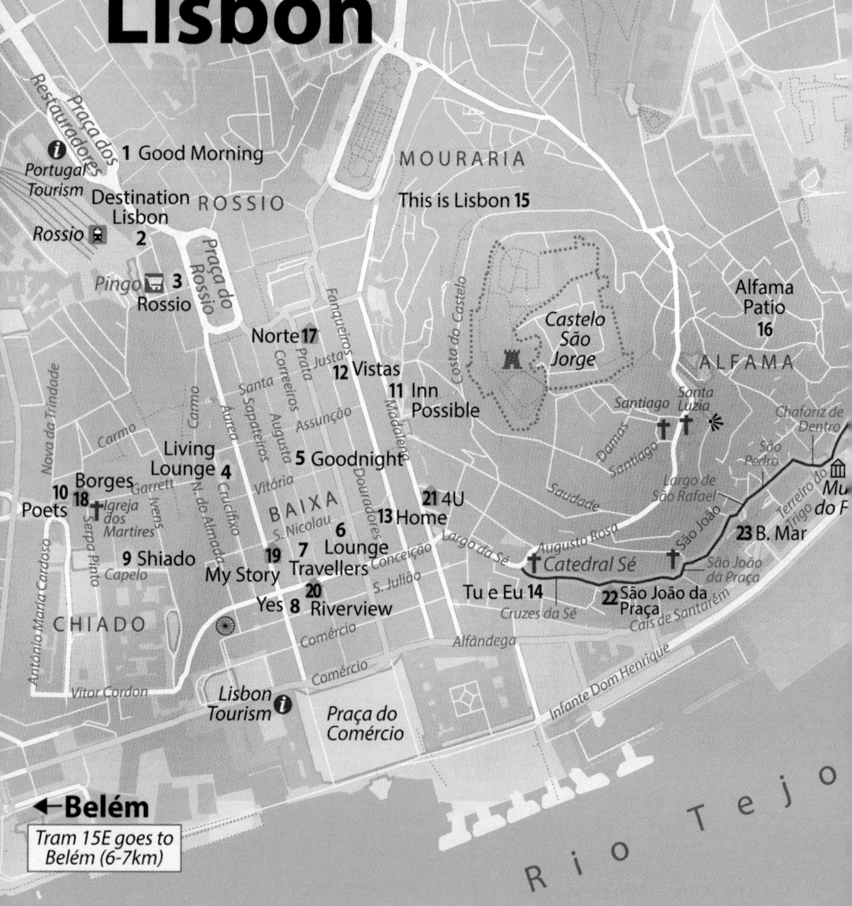

The first yellow arrow is on the bottom right side the Sé Cathedral (when facing the cathedral). Navigating out of Lisbon can be tricky. Pay close attention to road signs and marks (following both yellow Santiago and blue Fátima marks) and walk generally parallel to the Rio Tejo with (after the Teatro Ibérico) the railroad on your L. Angle back to the Tejo after passing through an underpass beside the railroad tracks (soon pass a hospital on your L) to reach the oceanarium and Parque das Nações and follow the Tejo until Rio Trancão. Follow the Trancão west to the north side of Sacavém (grocery off-route); cross to the north side of the Trancão along N-10; and follow dirt paths and roads north along the Trancão before leaving the river and joining a paved road near Granja.

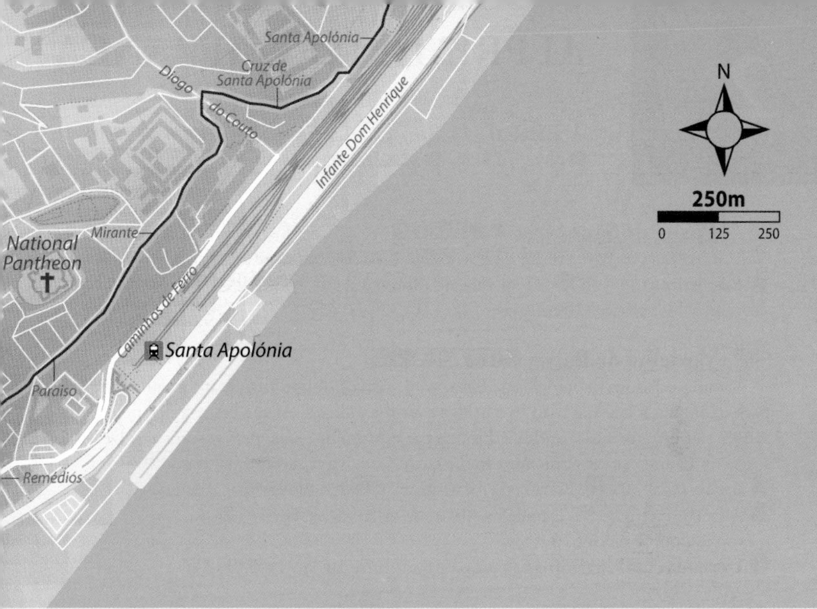

0.0 **Lisbon** A H

1. A H **Good Morning** (€22/-/65): , Praça dos Restauradores 65, 213421128
2. A H **Destination Lisbon** (€20-24/38/68): , Largo Duque do Cadaval 17, 213466457
3. A H **Rossio Hostel** (€16+/-/50): , Calda do Carmo 6, 213426004
4. A H **Living Lounge** (€18-22/35/52+): , Crucifixo 116, 213461078
5. A H **Goodnight Hostel** (€17+/-/66+): , Correeiros 113, 215989153
6. A H **Lounge Hostel** (€18-22/-/66+): , São Nicolau 41, 213462061
7. A H **Travellers House** (€21-25/35/70+): , Augusta 89, 210115922
8. A H **Yes! Lisbon Hostel** (€12-15/-/50): , São Julião 148, 213427171
9. A H **Shiado Hostel** (€17-19/-/54): , Anchieta 5, 213429227
10. A H **Poets Hostel** (€22/-0/50+): , Nova da Trindade 2, 213461241
11. A H **Inn Possible** (€15-18/-/70): , Regedor 3, 218861465
12. A H **Vistas de Lisboa** (€12+/-/45+): , Douradoures 178, 218867256
13. A **Home Lisbon** (€24-28): , São Nicolau 13, 218885312
14. A **Tu e Eu** (€20): , Escadinhas da Porta do Mar 3,
15. A H **This is Lisbon** (€15-17/-/50+): , Costa do Castelo 63, 218014549
16. A H **Alfama Patio** (€23-26/-/70): , Escola Gerais 3, Patio dos Quintalinhos 1, 218883127
17. H **Norte Guest House** (€40+): , Douradores 159, 962 129878
18. H **Borges** (€120+): , Garrett 108, 210456400
19. H **My Story Hotel** (€97/107+): , Áurea 100, 213400340
20. H **Riverview Hostel** (€50+): , Conceição 107, 962129878
21. H **Hostel 4U** (€80): , Madalena 96, 218874204
22. H **Pensão São João da Praça** (€35+): , São João da Praça 97, 218862591
23. H **B. Mar** (€60): , Largo Terreiro do Trigo 16, 218872181 ,

2 ALPRIATE TO VIAFRANCA

19.0km (11.8mi), 5-6 Hours, Difficulty:
P 68%, 12.9km, U 32%, 6.2km

3.7 Póvoa de Santa Iria

Most services in Póvoa de Santa Iria, except for a few cafés, are significantly off-route.

A **Bombeiros** (don): , Dom Vicente Afonso Valente 1, 219590032, cots and floor space, +800m

8.7 Verdelha de Baixo

Accommodations in Verdelha de Baixo are 1.4km off-route. Turn R at the end of the linear park, climbing a curving road to a bridge over the railroad. At the first traffic circle (Jumbo service station), turn L. Continue through the next traffic circle; pass grocery and Decathlon stores on L; and turn R at the next traffic circle to arrive at accommodations.

H **A Faia** (€20/30): , Estrada da Alfarrobeira 1, 934406967

H **Alfa 10** (€21/37): , Estrada da Alfarrobeira 10, 219580475, extra in double room €16

H **Dormidas Leal** (€15/30): Estrada da Alfarrobeira 10, 219585902

14.8 Alhandra

A **Bombeiros** (5, don): , Largo Bombeiros Voluntários, 219500021, cots and floor space

19.0 Vila Franca de Xira

1. A H **Domus Plaza** (€15/-/40): , António Palha 2, 926070650
2. A H **Vilatejo** (€15/30): , Praia 2a, 263272991, pension with singles, doubles and triples; pilgrim rate of €15 per person regardless of room
3. H **Hospedaria Maioral** (€25+): Travessa do Terreirinho 2, 263274370
4. H **Flora** (€30): , António Palha 2, 926070650
5. H **Leziria** (€50): , Barranco de Cegos 22, 263276670, +500m

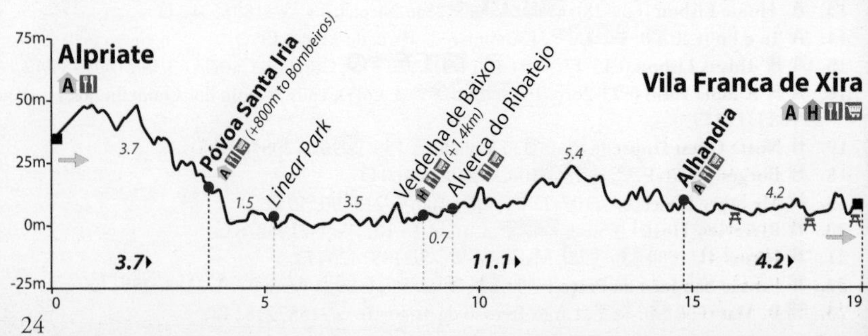

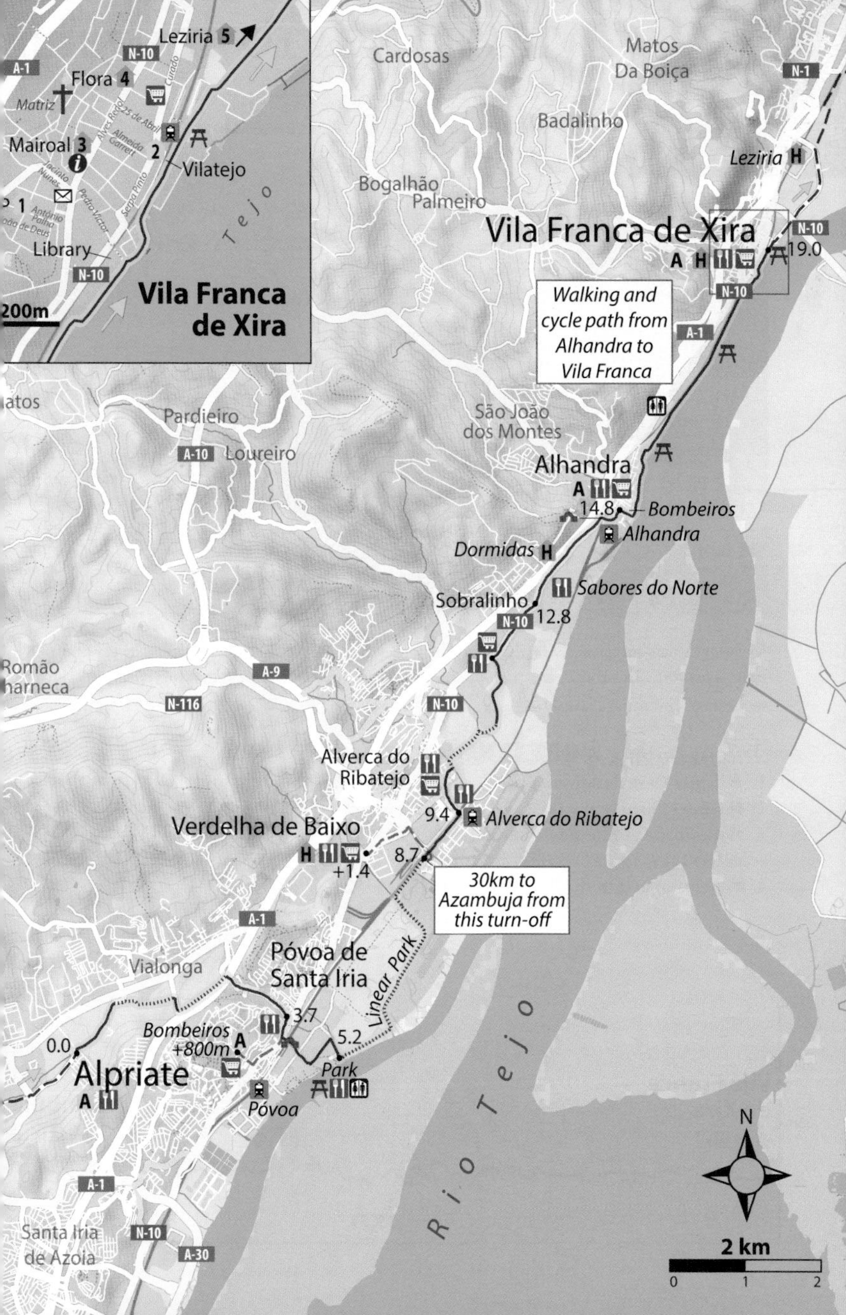

Vila Franca de Xira
Leziria 5
Flora 4
Matriz
Mairoal 3
1
2
Vilatejo
Library
Tejo
200m
N-10
A-1
Cardosas
Matos Da Boiça
Badalinho
Leziria
Bogalhão
Palmeiro
Vila Franca de Xira
19.0
Walking and cycle path from Alhandra to Vila Franca
Pardieiro
Loureiro
A-10
São João dos Montes
Alhandra
14.8
Bombeiros
Alhandra
Dormidas
Sabores do Norte
Sobralinho
12.8
Romão
A-9
N-116
Alverca do Ribatejo
9.4
Alverca do Ribatejo
Verdelha de Baixo
+1.4
8.7
30km to Azambuja from this turn-off
Póvoa de Santa Iria
Linear Park
Vialonga
3.7
5.2
Bombeiros +800m
0.0
Alpriate
Park
Póvoa
Rio Tejo
Santa Iria de Azoia
A-30
N
2 km
0
1
2

3 VILAFRANCA TO AZAMBUJA

19.7km (12.2mi), 5-6.5 Hours, Difficulty:
P 61%, 12.0km, U 39%, 7.7km

From Vila Franca de Xira the route becomes progressively more rural and the walking more pleasant. The route still runs parallel to commuter train lines, making it easy to skip sections of the route if desired.

19.7 Azambuja

1. **Santa Casa da Misericórdia** (par, 14, don): Espírito Santo 1, 914103807
2. **Hotel Ouro** (€35): E.N.3 Km 10, 263406530
3. **Residencial Flor da Primavera** (€25/35): Conselheiro Francisco Arouca 19, 263402545, 967067381, triple rooms €45
4. **Pensão Jacinto** (€20): Campinos 3c, 263402504, 965535677

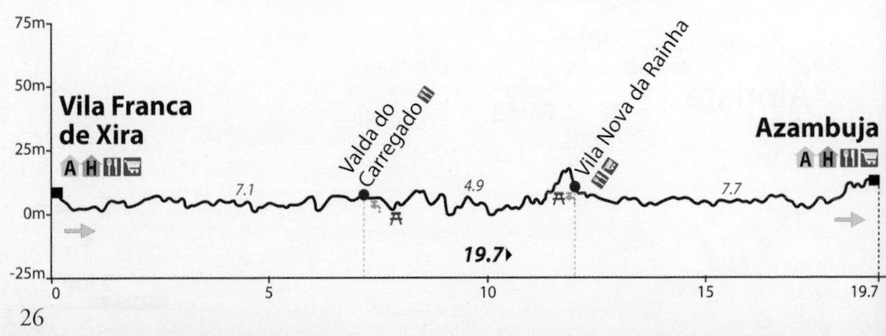

Sta. Casa da Misericórdia
4 Jacinto
Campinos
Espírito Santo
1
Health Center
3
Flor da Primavera
Valverde
Dom Rolim
N-3
Aldi
2 Ouro
200m
Azambuja
Next accommodation after Azambuja (in Valada): 12.9km
N-3
Azambuja
A H
19.7
18.6
Azambuja
N-1
A-1
N-3
Espadanal da Azambuja
Vila Nova da Rainha
12.0
Vila Nova da Rainha
Carregado
A-10
N-1
N-115-4
7.1
Vala do Carregado
A-10
Rio Tejo
Castanheira do Ribatejo
4.4
A-1
Simtejo Factory
0.0
Vila Franca de Xira
A H
N-10
Frequent commuter trains allow for skipping walking sections if desired.
N
2 km
0
1
2

4

AZAMBUJA TO SANTARÉM

32.5km (20.2mi), **8-11 Hours, Difficulty:**
P 57%, 18.6km, U 43%, 13.9km

A welcome change of pace from urban walking. Services fewer and farther between with no food or water over the last 16km. Stock up in Porto do Muge. Note the steep ascent at stage end.

12.9 Valada

1. **Casas de Valada** (8, €15): Santo Antonio 3, 919268039, call
2. **Salão Parochial** (par, don): Largo da Igreja, 914337000, floor space only, call

16.6 Porto do Muge

Cafe closes at 6pm.

Quinta da Burra (10, €20): Sabugueiro 177, 939997657

Casa do Rio (8, €15): Morgado 2, 919268039, call in advance

32.5 Santarém

The routes to Santiago and Fátima split on the east side of of Largo Cândido dos Reis (center circle). Buses run regularly between Santarém and Fátima.

⚠ Note that the Santarém city map is rotated 90 degrees left, with east upward.

1. **Santa Casa da Misericórdia** (24, €5): Largo Cândido dos Reis, 243305260, shared twin rooms, after 6pm enter at back gate, locked overnight
2. **Santarém Hostel** (24, €15/30/40): Engenheiro Antonio Antunes Junior 26, 965832702
3. **N1 Hostel** (64, €18/50/75): Combatentes 80, 243350140
4. **Casa das Flores** (€50): Pedro Canavarro 9, 243324101, €5 per additional person in apartment (up to 4 people total)
5. **Arminda** (€30): Frois 14, 243110079
6. **Vitória** (€25/45): Segundo Visconde Santarém 21, 243309130
7. **Casa do Arco** (€50): S. Martinho 30, 919235751
8. **Alcáçova** (€115-155/135-175): Dos Combatentes 80, 243350140
9. **Pensão Coimbra** (€15/25-35): 31 de Janeiro 44, 243322816
10. **Tagus Host** (€25/37+): D. Afonso Henriques, 79-A , 3, 913476949

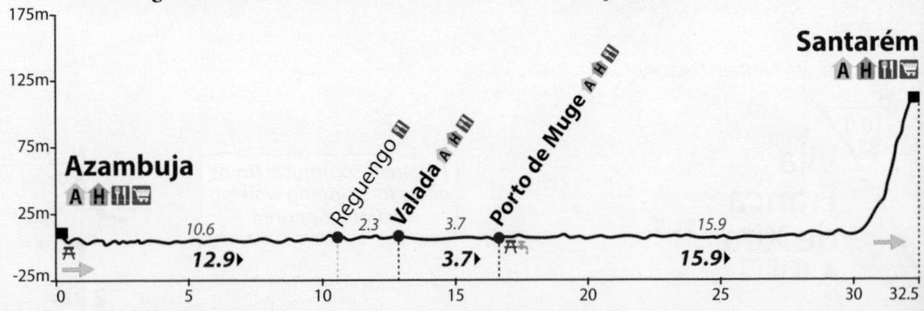

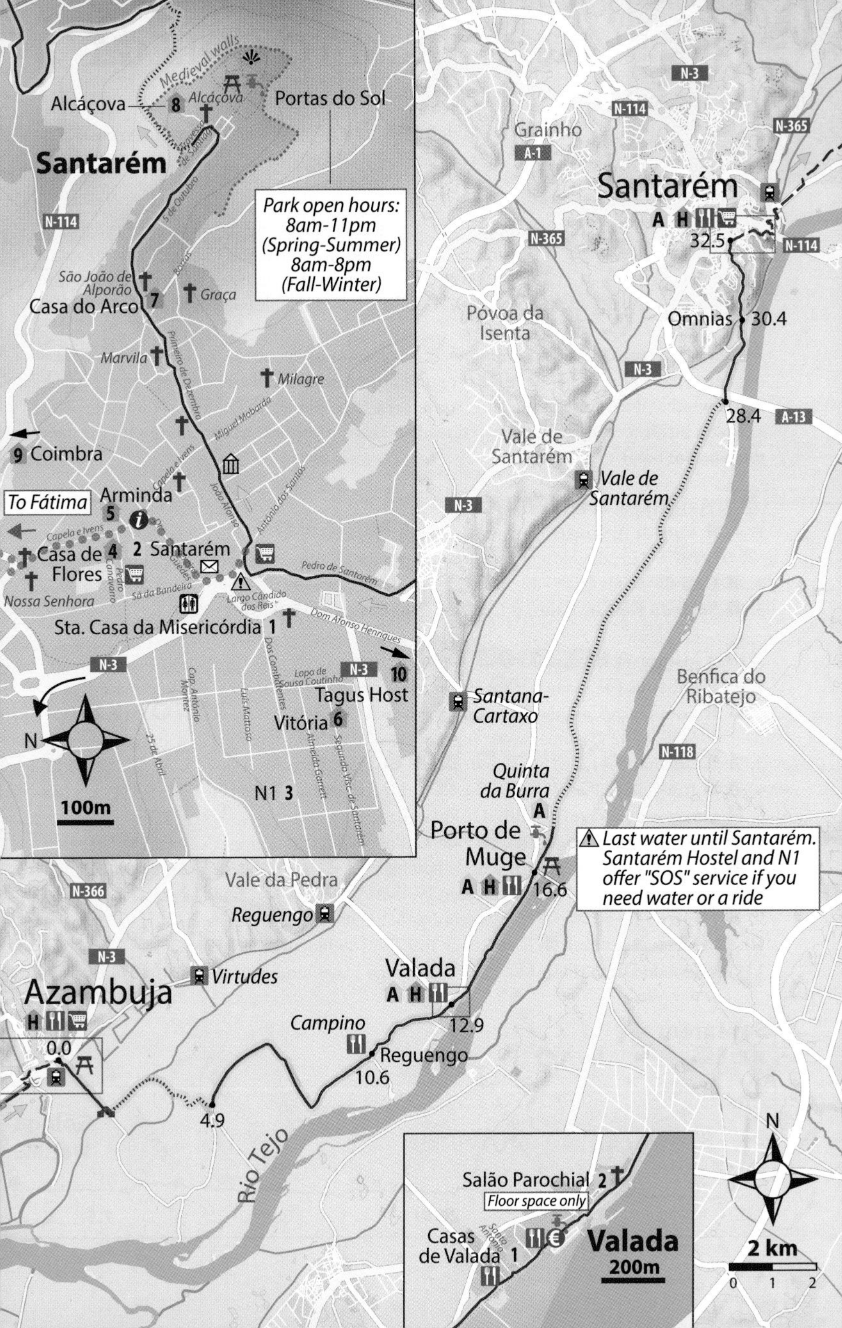

Medieval walls
Alcáçova
Alcáçova 8
Portas do Sol
Santarém
N-114
Park open hours:
8am-11pm
(Spring-Summer)
8am-8pm
(Fall-Winter)
São João de Alporão
Casa do Arco 7
Graça
Marvila
Milagre
9 Coimbra
To Fátima
Arminda
5
Casa de Flores 4
2 Santarém
Nossa Senhora
Sta. Casa da Misericórdia 1
N-3
10
Tagus Host
Vitória 6
N1 3
100m
N
N-3
N-114
Grainho
N-365
A-1
Santarém
A H
32.5
N-114
Póvoa da Isenta
Omnias 30.4
N-3
28.4
A-13
Vale de Santarém
Vale de Santarém
N-3
Santana-Cartaxo
Benfica do Ribatejo
N-118
Quinta da Burra
A
Porto de Muge
A H
16.6
Last water until Santarém. Santarém Hostel and N1 offer "SOS" service if you need water or a ride
N-366
Vale da Pedra
Reguengo
N-3
Virtudes
Azambuja
H
Valada
A H
Campino
12.9
0.0
Reguengo
10.6
4.9
Rio Tejo
Salão Parochial 2
Floor space only
Casas de Valada 1
Valada
200m
N
2 km
0 1 2

5 SANTARÉM TO GOLEGÃ

34.4km (21.4mi), 8.5-11.5 Hours, Difficulty:
P 53%, 18.2km, U 47%, 16.3km

Consider splitting this long stage (34.4km) and the following (30.7km) into three days: 1) Santarém to Azinhaga (26.9km); 2) Azinhaga to São Caetano (13.4km), Vila Nova da Barquinha (16.4km), or Atalaia (18.9km); 3) remainder to Tomar. Buses run regularly between Golegã and Azinhaga, so you can skip 7.5km of relatively unpleasant walking along N-365.

Consult the map for shortcut options such as continuing along the Tejo River (before turning northwest to Reguengo de Alviela) on faint dirt tracks directly to Azinhaga (not passable in wet weather due to risk of flooding), or skirting Pombalinho and Azinhaga (at Ponte Sobre a Alverca picnic area, turn L on a paved road and head northeast, reconnecting with the main route before Brôa).

26.9 Azinhaga A H

1. A H **Casa de Azzancha** (5, €20/-/40): Combatentes 80, 919187773, double and triple rooms; pilgrims €20/person; special meals for pilgrims
2. H **Casa da Azinhaga** (€70+): Misericórdia 26, 249957146
3. H **Solar do Espirito Santo** (€65+): Espirito Santo 25, 243110079

34.4 Golegã A H

1. A **Bombeiros** (5, don): Parque de Campismo, 249979070, floor space
2. A H **Solo Duro/Casa da Tia Guida** (6+, €10-15/-/40-50): José Relvas 84, 249976802, same owner, luggage transfer to/from Santarém and Tomar
3. A H **Ademas** (12, €15/-/30): Fred. Bon. dos Anjos 35, 918310195
4. A H **Inn Golegã** (12, €20/-/35): Dr Raf. da Cunha Franco 17, 933493397
5. H **Quartos do Lagar** (€15/20): Dr Rafael da Cunha Franco 17, 917591833
6. H **Pátio Avó Faustina** (€70+): Carlos Mendes Gonçalves 15 , 249977480
7. H **Lusitanus** (€40+): Marquês de Pombal 25, , 249977572, equestrian center
8. H **Cavalo Branco** (€44+): D. Joao IV, 249979003
9. H **Lusitano** (€100): Gil Vicente 4, 308807110
10. H **O Té** (€10/20/30): José Relvas 119, 918598820, 249976404
11. H **Casa do Largo** (€60+): Largo 5 de Outubro 15, 249104850

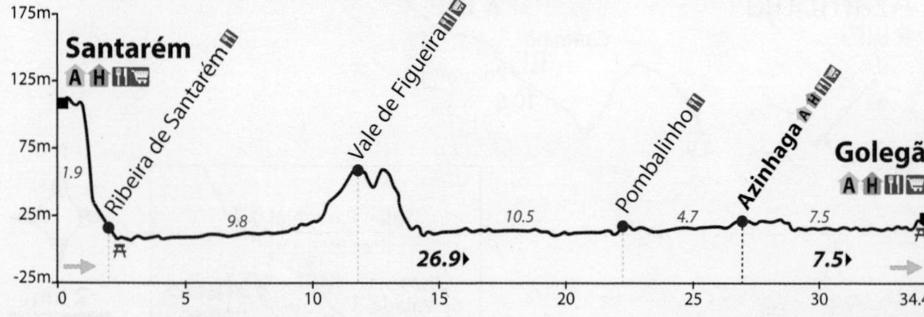

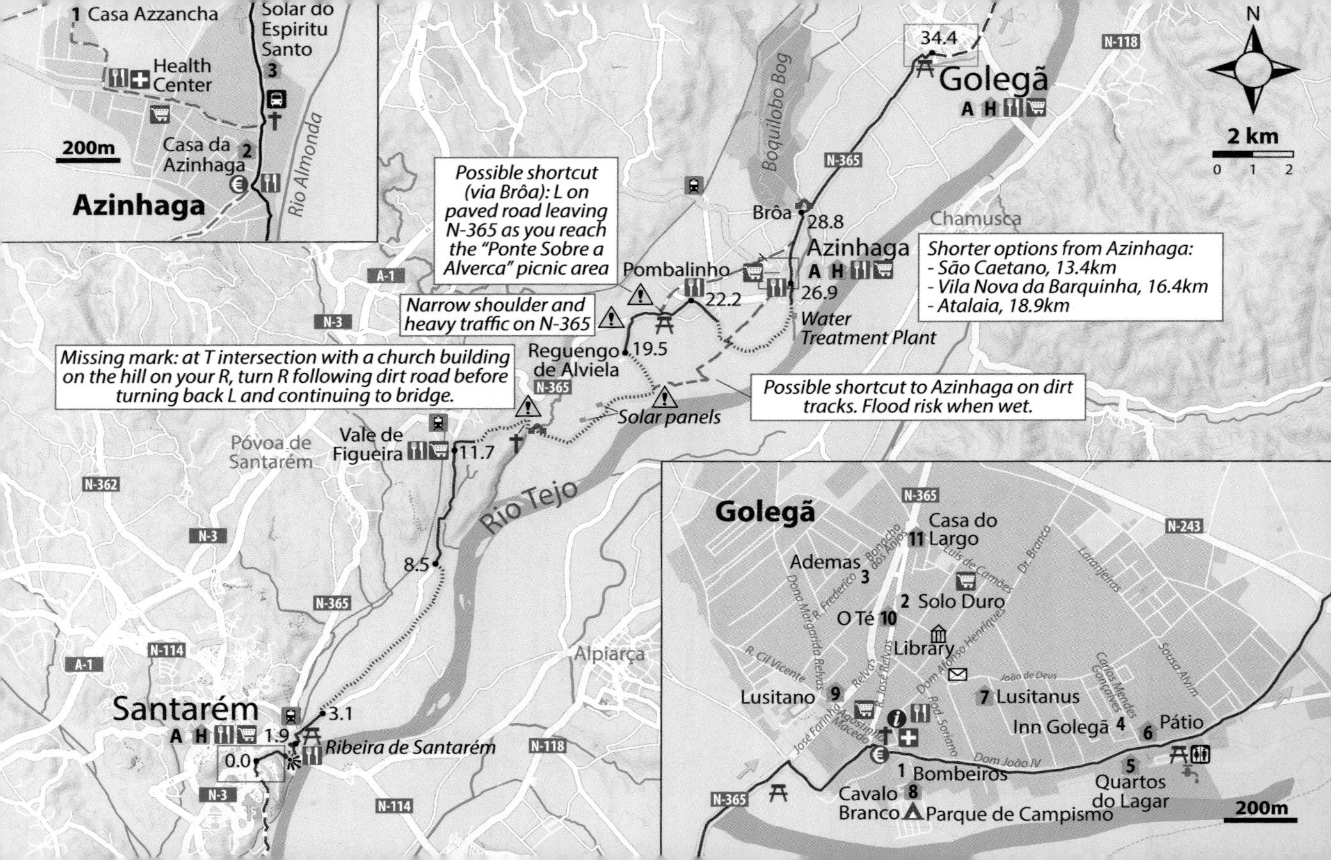

Possible shortcut (via Brôa): L on paved road leaving N-365 as you reach the "Ponte Sobre a Alverca" picnic area
Shorter options from Azinhaga:
- São Caetano, 13.4km
- Vila Nova da Barquinha, 16.4km
- Atalaia, 18.9km
Narrow shoulder and heavy traffic on N-365
Missing mark: at T intersection with a church building on the hill on your R, turn R following dirt road before turning back L and continuing to bridge.
Possible shortcut to Azinhaga on dirt tracks. Flood risk when wet.
Golegã
Azinhaga
Santarém
Brôa
Pombalinho
Reguengo de Alviela
Vale de Figueira
Póvoa de Santarém
Ribeira de Santarém
Chamusca
Alpiarça
Boquilobo Bog
Rio Tejo
Water Treatment Plant
Solar panels
34.4
28.8
26.9
22.2
19.5
11.7
8.5
3.1
1.9
0.0
2 km
0 1 2
N
Azinhaga
200m
1 Casa Azzancha
Health Center
2 Casa da Azinhaga
3 Solar do Espiritu Santo
Rio Almonda
Golegã
200m
1 Bombeiros
2 Solo Duro
3 Ademas
4 Inn Golegã
5 Quartos do Lagar
6 Pátio
7 Lusitanus
8 Cavalo Branco
9 Lusitano
10 O Té
11 Casa do Largo
Library
Parque de Campismo

6 GOLEGÃ TO TOMAR

30.7km (19.1mi), 7.5-10 HOURS, DIFFICULTY:
P 72%, 22.0km, U 28%, 8.7km

A long but varied walk including the village of São Caetano, flower-lined lanes of Quinta Cardiga, and eucalyptus forest, as well as less scenic populated areas, including 1.4km along highway N-110. The way is well-marked through the eucalyptus forest, all the way to Grou, but keep a close eye out for marks as it's not hard to get lost. There are several intermediate accommodation options today.

6.0 **São Caetano** A H
A H **Casa de São Caetano** (€20/-/40): 914951076, luggage transfer

8.9 **Vila Nova da Barquinha** H Train station just off-route, most services +1.2km off-route in town center. Almourol Castle is +4km east along the Tejo River.
H **Soltejo** (€26/40): N3, 249720150
H **Nature House/Art Inn** (€48+/60+): Primeiro de Dezembro 4, 918735242
H **Sonetos de Tejo** (€60+): Tejo 22, 249716194

11.4 **Atalaia** H
H **Casa do Patriarca** (€25/45): Patriarca Dom José 134, 249710581

30.7 **Tomar** A H Marked route to Fátima leaves Tomar, west around the north side of the Tomar Castle and Convento de Cristo. Regular Tomar-Fátima buses. ⚠ Note that the Tomar city map is rotated 90 degrees left, with east upward.

1. A H **2300 Thomar** (€15/-/35): Serpa Pinto 43, 249324256
2. A **Bombeiros** (don): Santa Iria, 249329140, several beds and floor space
3. H **Trovador** (€25+/40+): 10 de Agosto de 1385 22, 249322567
4. H **Thomar Story Guesthouse** (€43/48): João Carlos Everard 53, 249327268
5. H **Resedencial Luz** (€19/30): Serpa Pinto 144, 249312317, brkfast for fee
6. H **União** (€35+/50+): Serpa Pinto 94, 249323161, +€15 for triple
7. H **Cavaleiros de Cristo** (€35/50): Alex. Herculano 7, 249321067
8. H **Sinagoga** (€30+/41+): Gil Avô 31, 249323083
9. H **Pensão Residencial Luanda** (€25/40): Marquês Tomar 15, 249323200

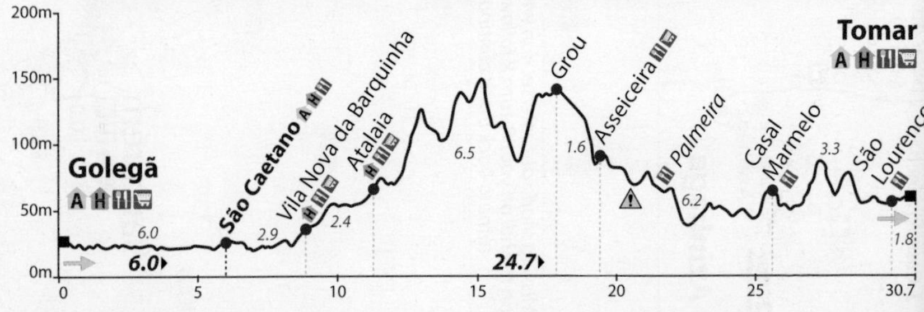

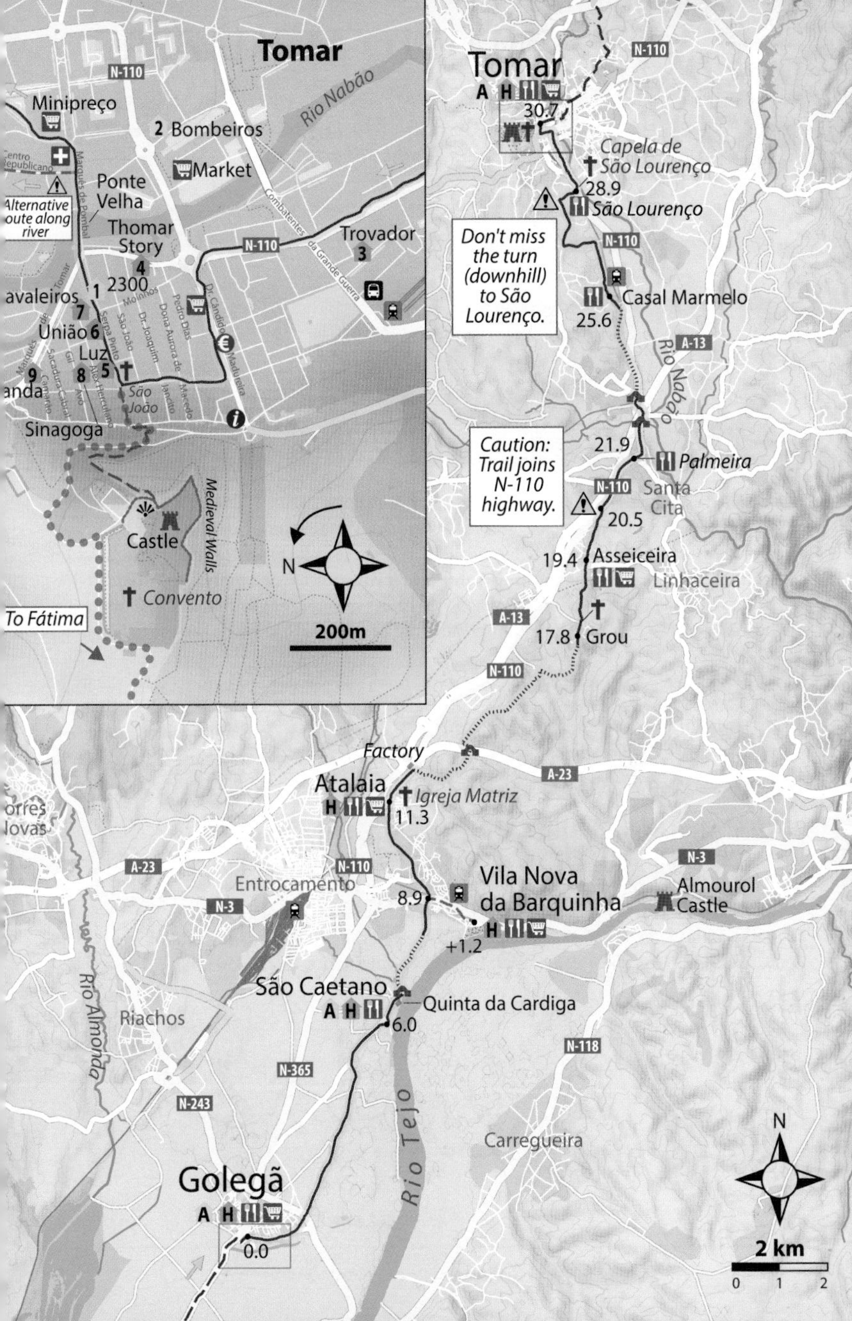

Tomar
N-110
Minipreço
2 Bombeiros
Rio Nabão
Market
Centro Republicano
Ponte Velha
Alternative route along river
Thomar Story
4
2300
Trovador
3
1
7
6
5
8
9
União
Luz
São João
Sinagoga
Castle
Medieval Walls
Convento
To Fátima
N
200m
Tomar
A H
30.7
Capela de São Lourenço
28.9
São Lourenço
Don't miss the turn (downhill) to São Lourenço.
N-110
Casal Marmelo
25.6
A-13
Rio Nabão
21.9
Palmeira
Caution: Trail joins N-110 highway.
Santa Cita
20.5
19.4
Asseiceira
Linhaceira
A-13
17.8
Grou
N-110
Factory
A-23
Atalaia
H
Igreja Matriz
11.3
Torres Novas
A-23
N-110
Entrocamento
N-3
8.9
Vila Nova da Barquinha
H
+1.2
N-3
Almourol Castle
São Caetano
A H
Quinta da Cardiga
6.0
Riachos
Rio Almonda
N-365
N-118
N-243
Rio Tejo
Carregueira
Golegã
A H
0.0
N
2 km
0 1 2

7

TOMAR TO ALVAIÁZERE

32.6km (20.3mi), 9-11.5 Hours, Difficulty:
P 74%, 24.2km, U 26%, 8.4km

Faded and infrequent marks make the exit from Tomar a bit challenging. Cross Ponte Velha and turn L after a pharmacy onto Rua Voluntários da República and pass a Minipreço on your R. Pay attention through residential areas, eventually passing a military barracks on your R and soon after angling L onto a dirt road leaving town. For a more scenic route, follow paths along the east bank of the Nabão River before reconnecting with the official route just before Peniche. (Be aware that this route may not be passable in wet weather due to flooding.)

Services are infrequent as you enter more rural, hilly terrain, so plan to carry plenty of water and food. There are cafés in Soianda and Calvinos. A service station 200m off-route in Tojal sells water and snacks. Some villages have fountains with signs noting that water is not potable. Pay attention before refilling your water; if unsure of water quality, refill at cafés or buy water at the service station.

32.6 **Alvaiázere** A H

1. A H **Residencial O Brás** (€15/-/30): W D, 15 de Maio 8, 236655405, hotel with pilgrim rate of €15 in shared double and triple rooms
2. A H **Albergaria Pinheiro's** (€12/15/20): K W D, Dr. Acúrsio Lopes 1, 915440196, 911150817, an ample breakfast for €2.50; amazing stamp!
3. A **Bombeiros** (6, don): Bombeiros Voluntários, 236650510

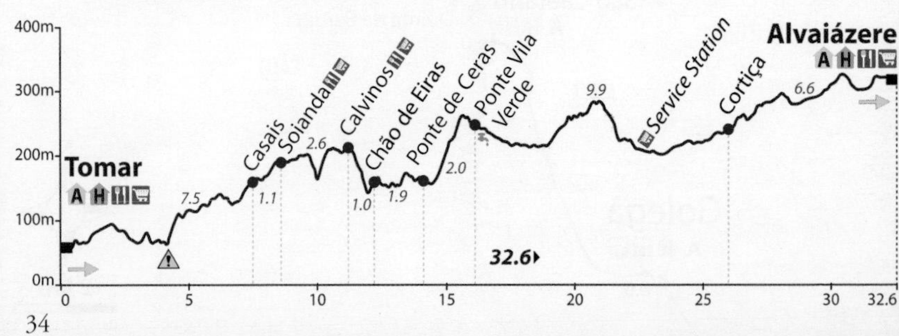

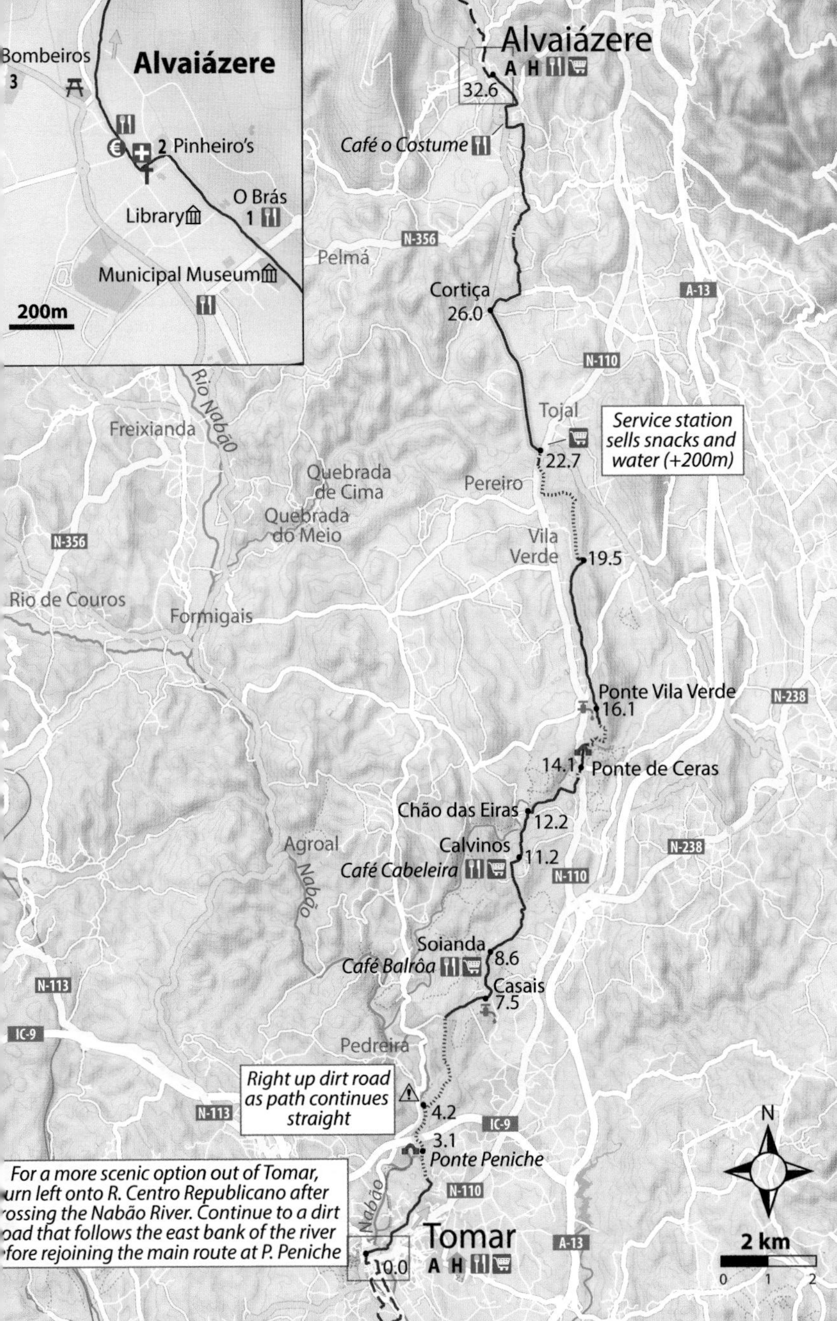

Alvaiázere
A H
32.6
Bombeiros
3
Alvaiázere
2 Pinheiro's
O Brás
1
Library
Municipal Museum
200m
Café o Costume
N-356
Pelmá
Cortiça
26.0
A-13
N-110
Rio Nabão
Tojal
Service station sells snacks and water (+200m)
22.7
Freixianda
Quebrada de Cima
Pereiro
Quebrada do Meio
Vila Verde
19.5
N-356
Rio de Couros
Formigais
Ponte Vila Verde
16.1
N-238
14.1
Ponte de Ceras
Chão das Eiras
12.2
Calvinos
11.2
N-238
Agroal
Nabão
Café Cabeleira
N-110
Soianda
8.6
Café Balrôa
Casais
7.5
N-113
IC-9
Pedreira
Right up dirt road as path continues straight
4.2
N-113
IC-9
3.1
Ponte Peniche
N
For a more scenic option out of Tomar, turn left onto R. Centro Republicano after crossing the Nabão River. Continue to a dirt road that follows the east bank of the river before rejoining the main route at P. Peniche
N-110
Nabão
Tomar
A-13
2 km
0.0
A H
0
1
2

8 ALVAIÁZERE TO RABAÇAL

31.8km (19.8mi), **8.5-11.5 Hours, Difficulty:**
45%, 14.4km, 55%, 17.4km

This is another beautiful day of walking through the forested hills of the Portuguese interior. Services are again sparse but sufficient. Anisão provides a convenient town for a break with restaurants, cafés, and grocery stores. To shorten what is otherwise a long, hilly day, Alvorge is a great place to spend the night and has a lovely albergue with a view. (If you stay in Alvorge, Cernache and its albergue are 26.4km away, followed by a short 12.4km day into Coimbra.)

After Alvaiázere the path once again follows the Fátima Route, but in reverse, so don't be confused by blue arrows.

13.0 Ansião A H

1. A H **Adega Típica** (8, €13/20/30): , Combatentes da Grande Guerra, 236677364, 919275851, 916149320, breakfast €5
2. A **Bombeiros** (4, €5): , Dr. Vitor Faveiro 16, 236670600
3. H **Solar da Raihna** (€25/35+): , Alto dos Pinherais, 236676204

22.9 Alvorge A

A **Albergue Parochial** (10, don): , Rua David Miguel Namora (in the lower floor of the Centro Paroquial), 913132477, very pleasant, simple, with a wonderful view; get the keys from Vitor at the café in the center square at the entrance to town

31.8 Rabaçal A H

1. A H **Albergue O Bonito** (16, €10/-/30): , Igreja, 916890599
2. A **Pousada Rabaçal (Casa do Tourismo)** (10, €15): Igreja, 918752990, 917620982, 239569371, 961631541 (English/Español), mixed reviews from pilgrims

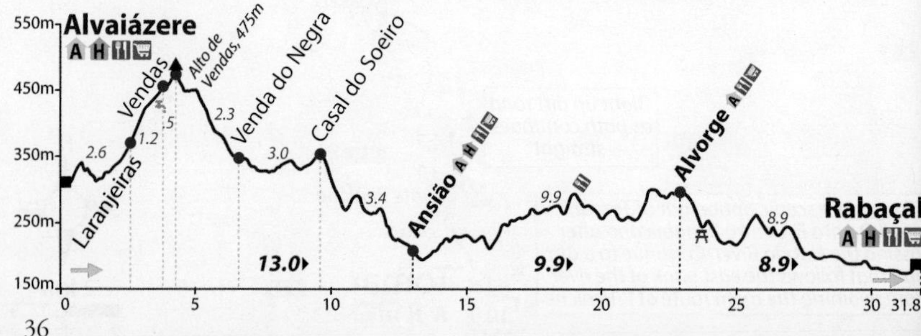

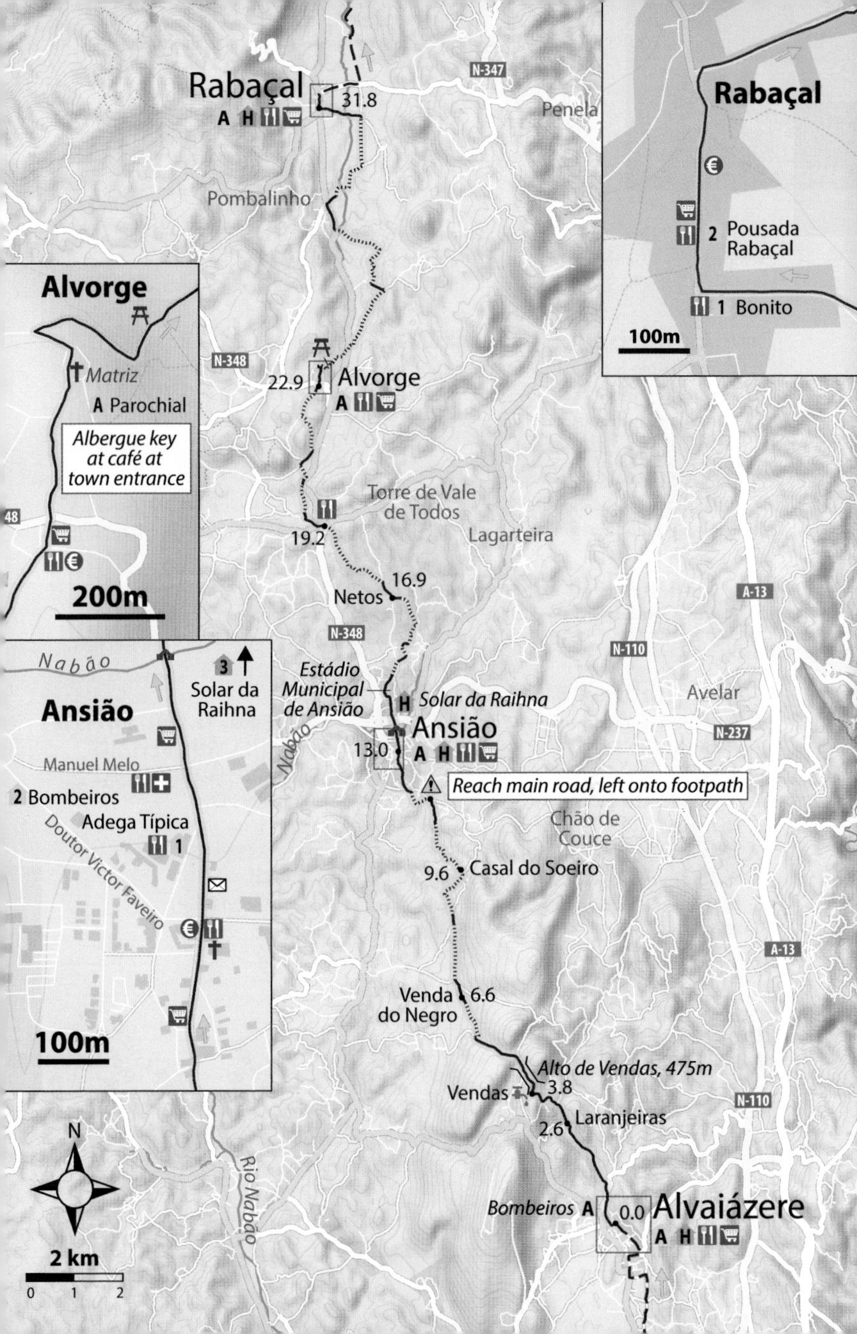

Rabaçal
A H
31.8
N-347
Penela
Pombalinho
N-348
22.9
Alvorge
A
Torre de Vale
de Todos
19.2
Lagarteira
16.9
Netos
N-348
Estádio
Municipal
de Ansião
H Solar da Raihna
Ansião
13.0
A H
Nabão
Reach main road, left onto footpath
Chão de
Couce
9.6
Casal do Soeiro
Venda
do Negro
6.6
Alto de Vendas, 475m
Vendas
3.8
Laranjeiras
2.6
Bombeiros A
0.0
Alvaiázere
A H
Rio Nabão
A-13
N-110
Avelar
N-237
A-13
N-110
N
2 km
0
1
2
Rabaçal
2 Pousada
Rabaçal
1 Bonito
100m
Alvorge
Matriz
A Parochial
Albergue key
at café at
town entrance
48
200m
Nabão
3
Solar da
Raihna
Ansião
Manuel Melo
2 Bombeiros
Adega Típica
1
Doutor Victor Faveiro
100m

9 RABAÇAL TO COIMBRA

28.9km (18.0mi), 7.5-10 HOURS, DIFFICULTY:
P 63%, 18.3km, U 37%, 10.6km

The first 11km continue through the countryside, which becomes progressively more developed near Coimbra. Conímbriga Roman ruins make a good lunch stop. For shorter stage options, Cernache and Santa Clara both have albergues as well as restaurants and shops.

+1.4 Condeixa a Nova

For Condeixa, turn L, leaving Camino at Café Triplo Jota (at 12km, after passing under N-347) and follow the road into town

Hospedes Ruínas (€25/35): D. M. E. Franco Sotto Mayor 35A, 239941772

Pousada Condeixa-Coimbra (€95): Francisco Lemos 43, 23994402

17.5 Cernache

1. A **Cernache** (asoc, 16, €8): Álvaro Anes 37, 968034708, 2-10p
2. A **Colegio da Imaculada Conceiçião** (40, don): 239940030, north in town

27.3 Santa Clara

A **Rainha Santa Isabel** (31, €10): Igreja Rainha Santa Isabel, 239441674, 2-10pm, check-in before 6:30pm, café with snacks & sandwiches

28.9 Coimbra

1. A H **Portagem Hostel** (22, €15/-/28+): Couraça Estrela 11, 917569143
2. A H **Hostel Sé Velha** (18+, €18/55): Norte 11/13, 916615577
3. A H **Serenata** (28, €18/-/49): Sé Velha 21, 239853130
4. H **Residencial Larbelo** (€38+): Portagem 33, 239829092
5. H **Avenida** (€27/35): Emídio Navarro 37, 239822155
6. H **Pensão Jardim** (€45-50): Emídio Navarro 65, 239825204
7. H **Ibis** (€38-43): Emídio Navarro 70, 239852130
8. H **Astoria** (€60+): Emídio Navarro 21, 239853020
9. H **Vitória** (€40-55/50-75): Sota 9, 239824049
10. H **Flor de Coimbra** (€40-45): Poço 5, 239823865

11-15. Continued on opposite page.

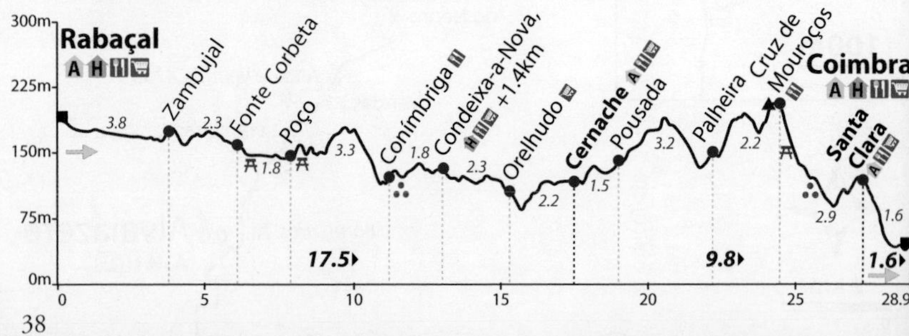

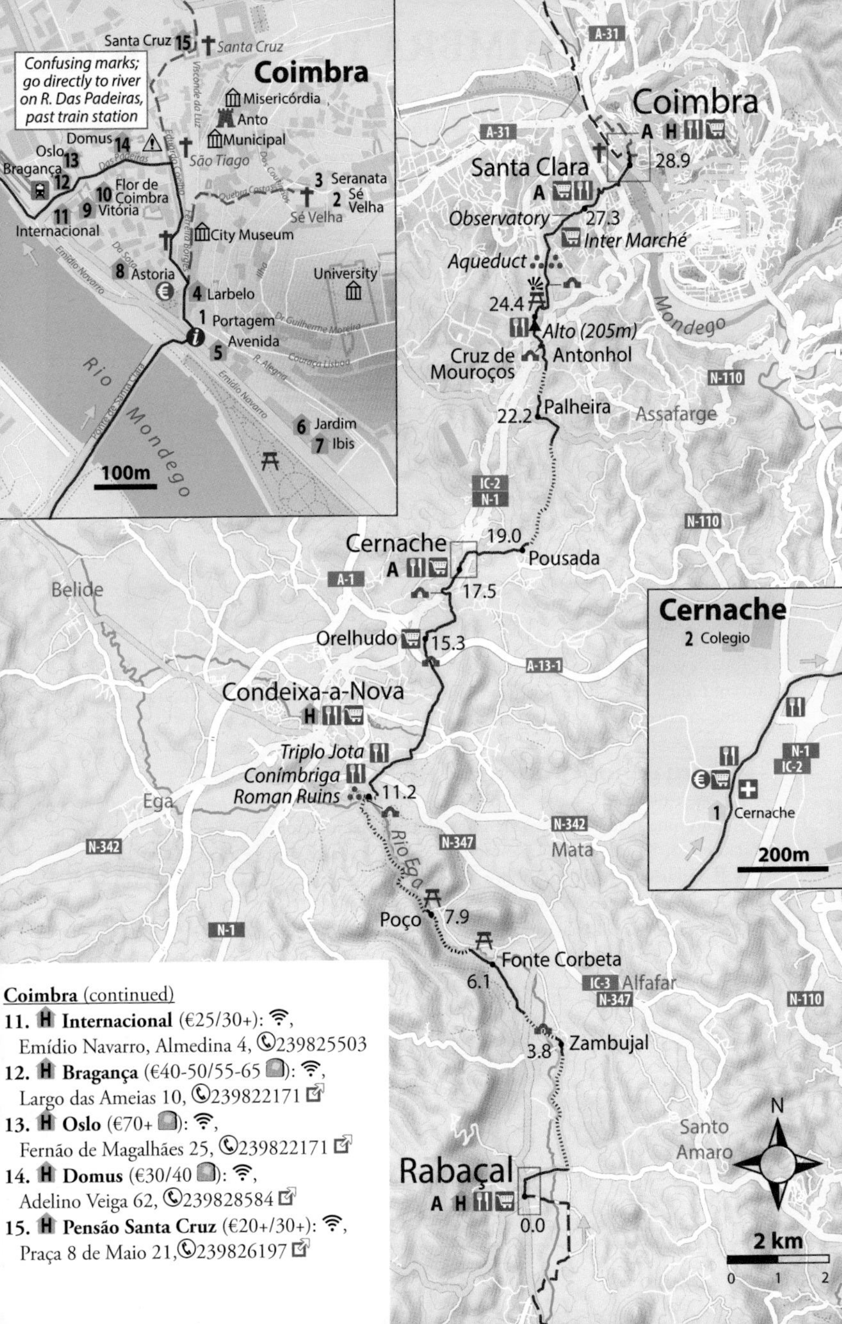

Coimbra (continued)

11. **H** **Internacional** (€25/30+): Emídio Navarro, Almedina 4, 239825503

12. **H** **Bragança** (€40-50/55-65): Largo das Ameias 10, 239822171

13. **H** **Oslo** (€70+): Fernão de Magalhães 25, 239822171

14. **H** **Domus** (€30/40): Adelino Veiga 62, 239828584

15. **H** **Pensão Santa Cruz** (€20+/30+): Praça 8 de Maio 21, 239826197

10 COIMBRA TO SERNADELO

24.8km (15.4mi), **6.5-8.5 Hours, Difficulty:**
P 87%, 21.5km, U 13%, 3.3km

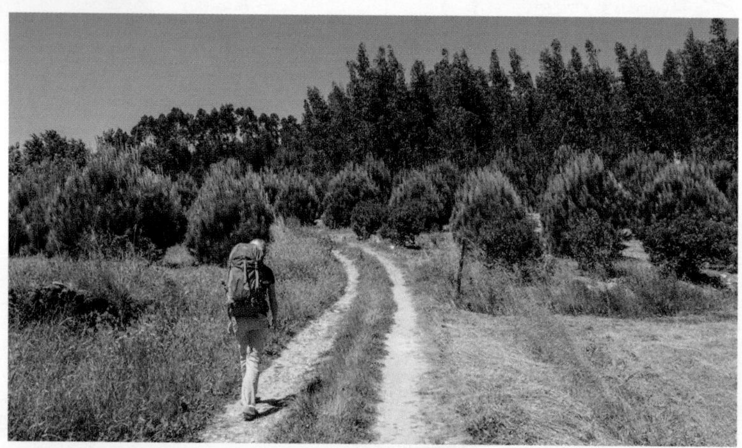

Today's walk leads through populated areas and along several busy roads. ⚠ Be extra cautious of traffic; walk on the left side of the road and be sure to check in all directions before crossing intersections. Avoid listening to headphones or other distractions.

24.8 Sernadelo/Mealhada

The stage distance is measured to Albergue Hilário in Sernadelo. Most services (grocery, restaurants, pharmacies, ATMs) are in Mealhada (1.5km before the albergue), while accommodations are located in the 1.5km following Mealhada, stretching to Sernadelo.

1. A H **Hilário** (16, €10/15/30): , Restauração 30, 914437715
2. H **Residencial Oásis** (€25/40): , Floresta 39, 231202081
3. H **Hotel dos Três Pinheiros** (€52): , Estrada Nacional 1, 231202391

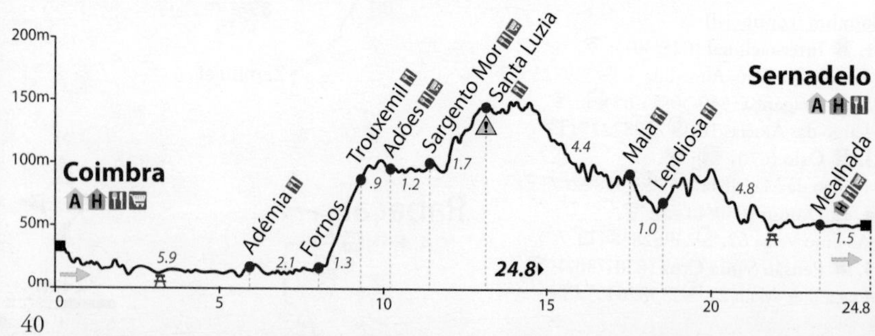

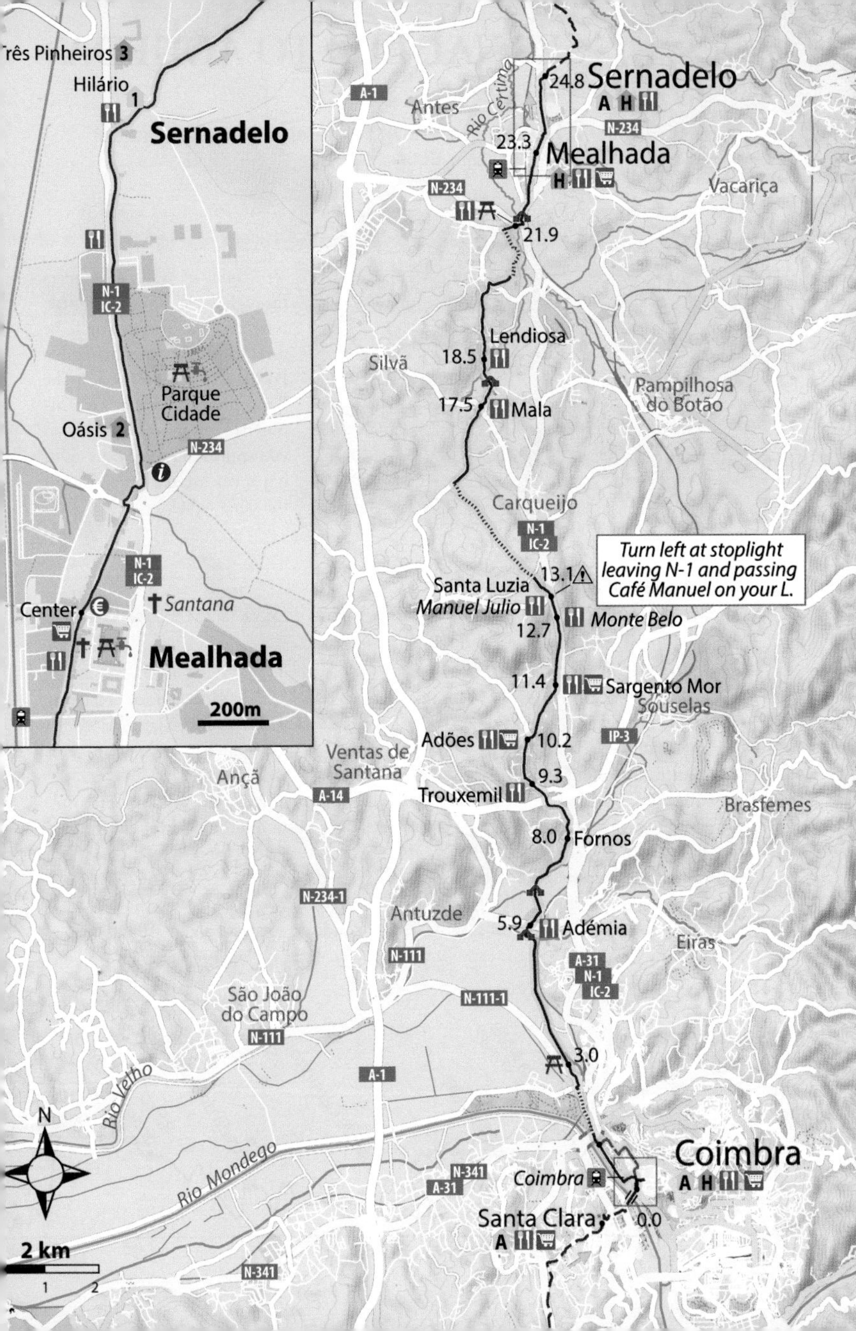

Três Pinheiros 3
Hilário 1
Sernadelo
N-1
IC-2
Parque
Cidade
Oásis 2
N-234
N-1
IC-2
Santana
Center
Mealhada
200m
24.8 Sernadelo
A H
Antes
Rio Certima
A-1
N-234
23.3 Mealhada
H
Vacariça
N-234
21.9
Lendiosa
18.5
Silvã
17.5 Mala
Pampilhosa
do Botão
Carqueijo
N-1
IC-2
Turn left at stoplight
leaving N-1 and passing
Café Manuel on your L.
13.1
Santa Luzia
Manuel Julio
Monte Belo
12.7
11.4
Sargento Mor
Souselas
IP-3
Adões
10.2
Ventas de
Santana
Ançã
9.3
A-14
Trouxemil
Brasfemes
8.0 Fornos
N-234-1
Antuzde
5.9 Adémia
Eiras
N-111
A-31
N-1
IC-2
N-111-1
São João
do Campo
N-111
3.0
A-1
Rio Velho
N
Rio Mondego
N-341
A-31
Coimbra
Coimbra
A H
Santa Clara
0.0
A
2 km
1
2
N-341

11

SERNADELO TO ÁGUEDA

23.6km (14.7mi), 6-8 Hours, Difficulty:
P 89%, 21.0km, U 11%, 2.6km

Today's walk meanders through little town after little town. In the spring you'll be sure to notice the incredible Portuguese flower beds. The Barró industrial zone is less attractive but passes quickly as you approach Águeda, an inviting town located on a river of the same name.

6.9 Anadia

H **Anadia Cabecinho** (€20/35/44): , Eng. Tavares da Silva, 231510940

23.6 Águeda

1. A H **XPT** (8, €20/35/44): , Vasco da Gama 37, 933571281, €3 for breakfast
2. A **Águeda Hostel and Friends** (40, €20-24): , José Maria Veloso 8, 911804490, 234136620
3. A **Santo António** (19, €12): , Av. da Misericordia 713, 234602871, all year, great vibe and wonderful garden; off-route (1.2km north on N-1), but the owners can give you directions back to the Camino route further north to avoid backtracking
4. H **Residencial Celeste** (€30/48): , Estrada Nacional 1, 234602871, same owners and location as Albergue Santo António
5. H **Conde d'Águeda** (€60/80): , Conde de Águeda, 234610390

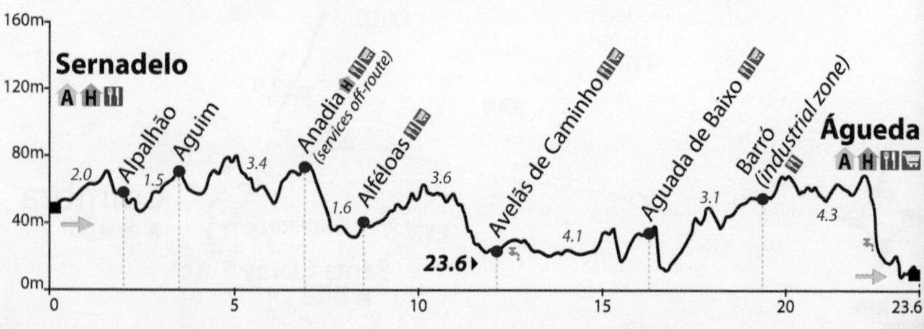

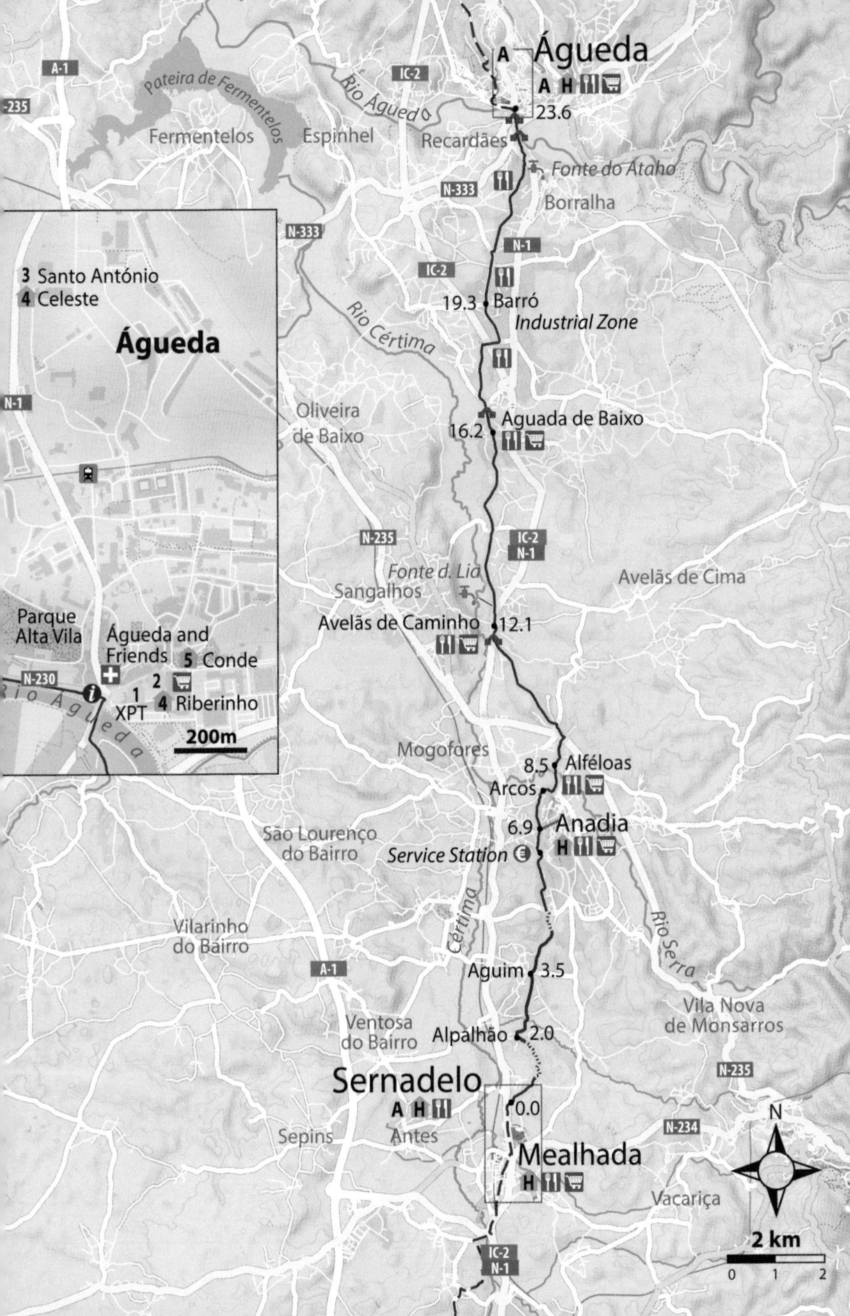

Águeda
A
A H
23.6
A-1
IC-2
-235
Rio Águeda
Pateira de Fermentelos
Fermentelos
Espinhel
Recardães
Fonte do Ataho
N-333
Borralha
N-333
N-1
IC-2
19.3 Barró
Industrial Zone
Rio Cértima
3 Santo António
4 Celeste
Águeda
N-1
Oliveira de Baixo
Aguada de Baixo
16.2
N-235
IC-2
N-1
Fonte d. Lia
Sangalhos
Avelãs de Cima
Parque Alta Vila
Águeda and Friends
5 Conde
Avelãs de Caminho
12.1
N-230
Rio Águeda
2
1
XPT
4 Riberinho
200m
Mogofores
8.5 Alféloas
Arcos
6.9 Anadia
H
São Lourenço do Bairro
Service Station
Cértima
Rio Serra
Vilarinho do Bairro
A-1
Aguim
3.5
Vila Nova de Monsarros
Ventosa do Bairro
Alpalhão
2.0
N-235
Sernadelo
A H
0.0
N-234
Sepins
Antes
Mealhada
H
Vacariça
N
2 km
0
1
2
IC-2
N-1

12 ÁGUEDA TO ALBERGARIA A NOVA

23.5km (14.6mi), 6-8 Hours, Difficulty:

P 71%, 16.8km, U 29%, 6.7km

After yet another industrial zone to start the day, the rest of the day passes through rural villages and along some stretches on dirt roads. The medieval bridge over a tributary of the Vouga River takes you back in time, and Albergaria a Velha—with its pleasant center and many services—is a nice place to take an extended break. There are fewer services in Albergaria a Nova, but ending there sets you up for a manageable walk to São João de Madeira the next day.

16.1 Albergaria a Velha A H

1. A **Rainha D. Teresa** (assoc, 21, €8): Bernardino Máximo de Albuquerque 14, 234529754, 2pm-10pm
2. H **Pensão Casa da Alameda** (€15/30): Bernardino Máximo de Albuquerque 2, 234524242
3. H **Pensao Restaurante Parentes** (€15+/30+): Dr. Brito Guimarães 11, 234521271, offers pilgrim menu
4. H **Hotel Alameda** (€25/35): EN n1 (IC 2), 234523402
5. H **Ribeirotel** (€40-50): Zona Industrial M566-1, 234524246

23.5 Albergaria a Nova A H

A H **Albergue Albergaria a Nova** (23, €10/-/25): Estrada Nacional 1, Km 252.3 #66, 234547068, Pleasant lodging run by a nice family; the owners shuttle pilgrims to the nearest grocery store (+900m) in the evening

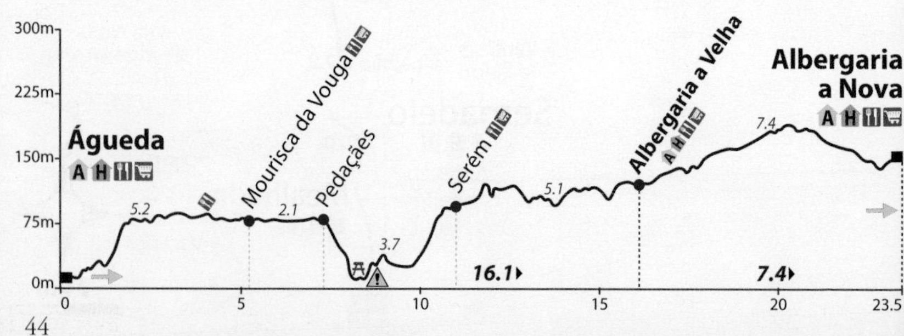

5 Ribeirotel
Albergaria a Velha
IC-2
N-1
Paroquial
Library
3 Parentes
Alameda 2
1 Rainha D. Teresa
Alameda 4
100m
Albergaria a Nova
23.5
A H
A Albergaria a Nova (900m before center)
22.6
N-1
IC-2
Santuário de Nossa Senhora do Socorro
19.7
Rio Caima
Ribeirotel H
N-16
Rio Vouga
16.1
Albergaria a Velha
A H
14.6
H Alameda
N-1
IC-2
A-25
A-1
Serém
11.0
Machinata do Vouga
Walk on highway to cross bridge
8.8
Roman Bridge
8.0
Pedaçães
7.3
Valongo do Vouga
Rio Vouga
5.2
Mourisca da Vouga
4.0
N-230
Industrial Zone
N-333
A Santo António
N
IC-2
Águeda
0.0
A H
Rio Agueda
2 km
N-333
N-1
0
1
2

13 ALBERGARIA A NOVA TO SÃO JOÃO DA MADEIRA

22.1km (13.7mi), 6-8 Hours, Difficulty:

P 97%, 21.4km, U 3%, 0.7km

5.4 Pinheiro da Bemposta

Moinho Garcia (10, €11-12): Garcia 322, 935500595, +1.5km

13.0 Oliveira de Azeméis

1. **Bombeiros** (don): Bombeiros Voluntários, 256682122, 256600670, not open all day; call in advance
2. **Dighton** (€55/60+): Largo da República, 256682191
3. **Pensão Restaurante Anacleto** (€15/30): Dr. António J Almeida 314, 256682541

22.1 São João de Madeira

1. **Santa Casa da Misericórdia** (par, don): Manuel Luis Leite Júnior 777, 256837240, floor space only
2. **Solar São João** (€35-50): Praça Luis Ribeiro 165, 256202540
3. **Hotel A.S. São João** (€35+): Praça Luis Ribeiro 7, 256836100
4. **Business Hotel** (€60+): Adelino Amaro da Costa 573, 256106700

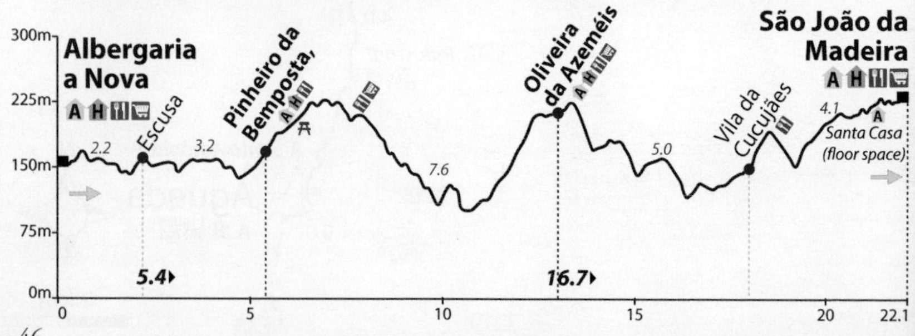

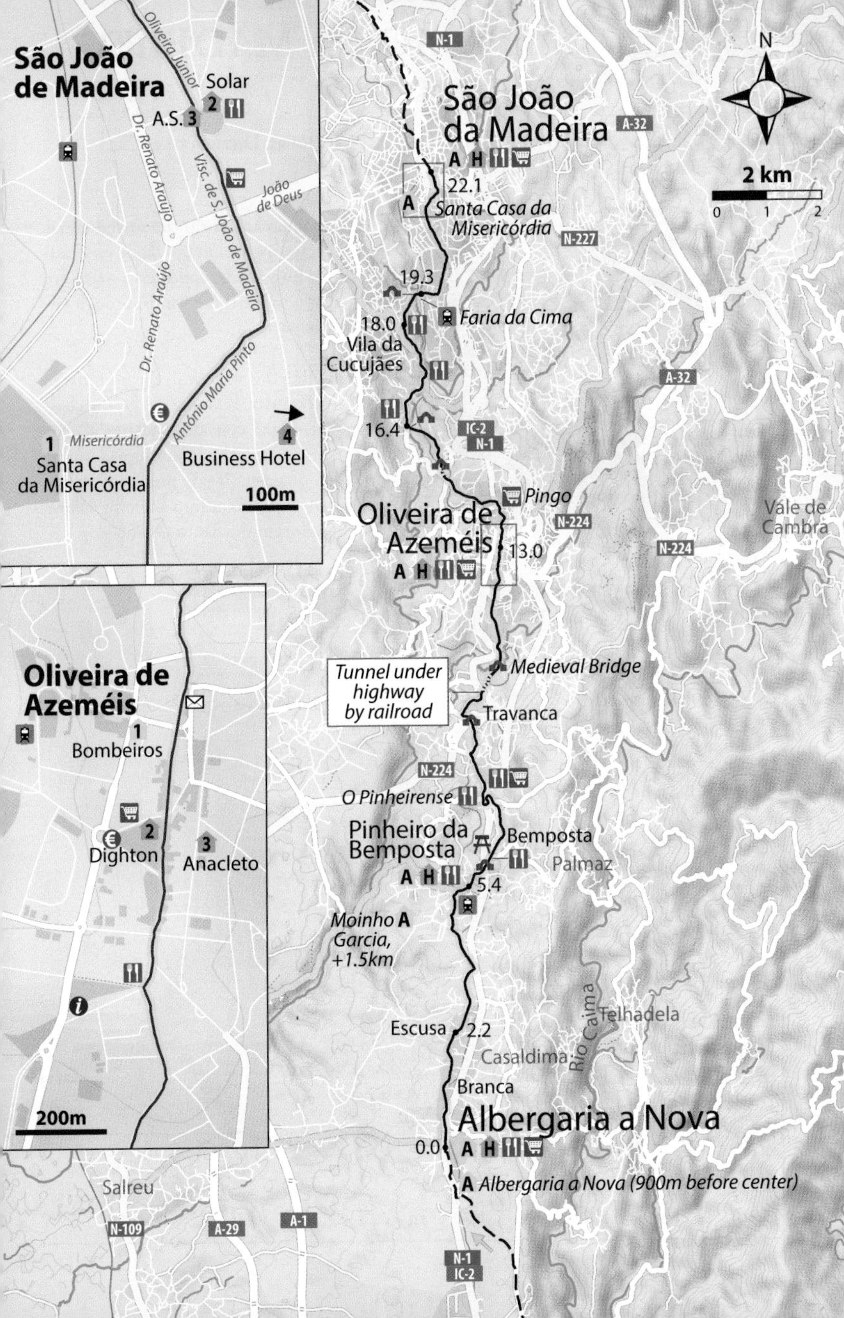

São João de Madeira
Oliveira Júnior
Solar
2
A.S. 3
Dr. Renato Araújo
Visc. de S. João de Madeira
João de Deus
António Maria Pinto
4
Business Hotel
1
Misericórdia
Santa Casa da Misericórdia
100m
Oliveira de Azeméis
1
Bombeiros
2
Dighton
3
Anacleto
200m
N-1
São João da Madeira
A-32
N
2 km
0 1 2
22.1
Santa Casa da Misericórdia
N-227
19.3
Faria da Cima
18.0
Vila da Cucujães
A-32
16.4
IC-2
N-1
Pingo
Oliveira de Azeméis
13.0
N-224
Vale de Cambra
N-224
Medieval Bridge
Tunnel under highway by railroad
Travanca
N-224
O Pinheirense
Pinheiro da Bemposta
Bemposta
Palmaz
5.4
Moinho Garcia, +1.5km
Rio Caima
Telhadela
Escusa
2.2
Casaldima
Branca
Albergaria a Nova
0.0
Albergaria a Nova (900m before center)
Salreu
N-109
A-29
A-1
N-1
IC-2

14 SÃO JOÃO DA MADEIRA TO GRIJÓ

18.6km (11.6mi), 5-6 Hours, Difficulty:
P 96%, 17.8km, U 4%, 0.8km

As you approach Porto the surroundings become increasingly built up. ⚠ Be very cautious along busy roads, and keep a sharp eye on waymarks as the route winds through villages and hamlets.

Combining this stage with the next makes a long 34.2km day. If you're up for the challenge, you might consider walking all the way to Porto to get the urban sprawl out of the way in one day. (If you need to, you can then cut the last 3.5km into Porto by taking the light rail from the Santo Ovídio stop.)

7.1 Malaposta

H **Pedra Bela** (€35-50): Malaposta 510, 256910350

18.6 Grijó

A **São Salvador de Grijó** (par, 28, €7): Cardoso Pinto 274, 968702769 , key at the house next to albergue to the west

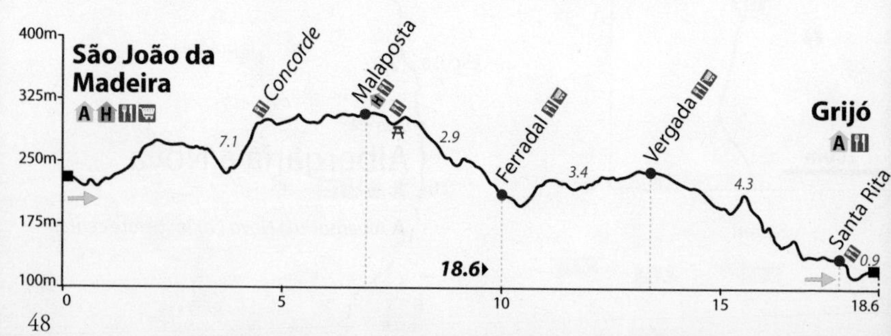

A-32
A-41
A-1
N-222
Seixezelo
Mosteiro São Salvador
18.6
Grijó
A
17.7
Capela Santa Rita
A-41
Guetim
Santa Rita
IC-2
N-1
Argoncilhe
A-32
A-41
Nogueira da Regedoura
Sanguedo
N-222
Vergada
13.4
N-223
Gião
N-326
Mozelos
Fiães
N-326
Lourosa
Ferradal
10.0
Industrial Area
Santa Maria de Lamas
Paços de Brandão
A-1
Guisande
IC-2
N-1
Caldas de São Jorge
N-223
A-29
Malaposta
Rio Meão
São João de Ver
Pigeiros
7.1
H
A-32
N-223
Sanfins
4.5
Concorde
N-223
Santa Maria da Feira
Espargo
Minipreço
Repsol Service Station
São João da Madeira
0.0
A
H
Santa Casa da Misericórdia
A
N-227
A-1
N
A-29
2 km
0
1
2
N-1
IC-2

15 GRIJÓ TO PORTO

15.6km (9.7mi), 4-5 Hours, Difficulty:
88%, 13.7km, 12%, 1.9km

Much of this stage traverses populated areas; exercise caution on busy roads and crossings. Just after Perosinho, a forested climb over the day's high point (236m) on the remains of a Roman road offers a pleasant interlude. As you approach Porto, navigation becomes more difficult—pay close attention at intersections. Once you reach the Santo Ovídio light rail station, follow the tram lines the rest of the way (mostly downhill) to the bridge over the Douro River. While you can descend to the level of the river before crossing, you'll then have to climb back up to the cathedral on the other side—best to simply cross the bridge on the upper level.

15.6 **Porto** A H City map on p. 52.

1. A **Albergue de Peregrinos** (26, €10): , Barão de Forrester 954, 220140515
2. A H **Bluesock Hostel** (€15-27/-/98): , São João 40, 227664171
3. A **Yes! Porto Hostel** (€17-20): , Arquitecto Nicolau Nasoni 31, 222082391
4. A H **Downtown Hostel** (37, €12-15/-/40): , Praça Guilherme Gomes Fernandes 66, 223234729 , all year
5. A H **Oporto Invictus Hostel** (€17-20/-/48): , Oliveiras 73, 222024371
6. A H **Gallery Hostel** (€25/-/75): , Miguel Bombarda 222, 224964313
7. A **ViaPortuscale** (assoc, 18, don): , Vasco Santana 264, 960227134
8. A **N.S. do Rosario de Vilar** (par, 18, €23): Arcediago Van Zeller 50 , 910274982
9. A **Igreja de Bonfim** (par, 8, €5): Monte do Bonfim 72, 225899690, must reserve
10. A H **Oporto Sport Hostel** (€11/-/28): , Santa Catarina 313, 916455958
11. A H **Spot Hostel** (€18-20/-/75): , Gonçalo Cristóvão 12, 224085205
12. A **City Drops Hostel** (€10-12): , Raúl Dória 11, 915423974
13. A H **República Hostel** (€22/-/100): Praça da República 38, 222011270
14. H **The Poets Inn** (€52-70): , Praça de Gomes Teixeira 7, 223324209
15. H **Peninsular** (€36/46): , Sá da Bandeira 21, 222003012
16. H **Pensão Franca** (€15/30): , Praça de Gomes Teixeira 7, 222002791
17. H **Vivacity** (€50-90): , Praça Guilherme Gomes Fernandes 35, 222085831
18. H **Lusitana** (€45/55): , Rosário 241, 222085851
19. H **Residencial Belo Sonho** (€28/38): Passos Manuel 186, 222003389
20. H **Del Norte** (€35/45): Fernandes Tomas 579, 222003503
21. H **Portuense Alojamento** (€30/35): , Rodolfo de Araújo 80, 914628757

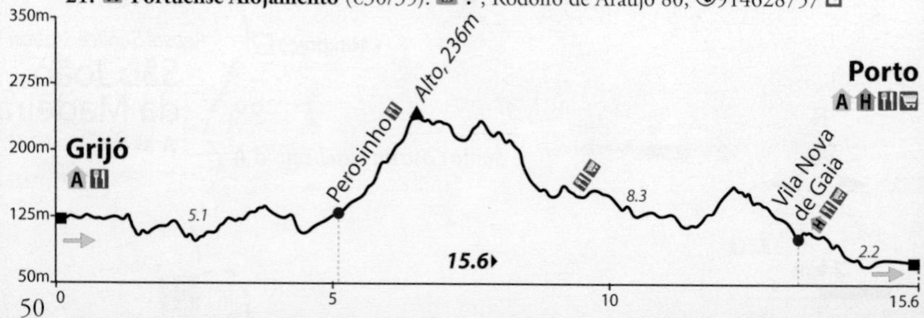

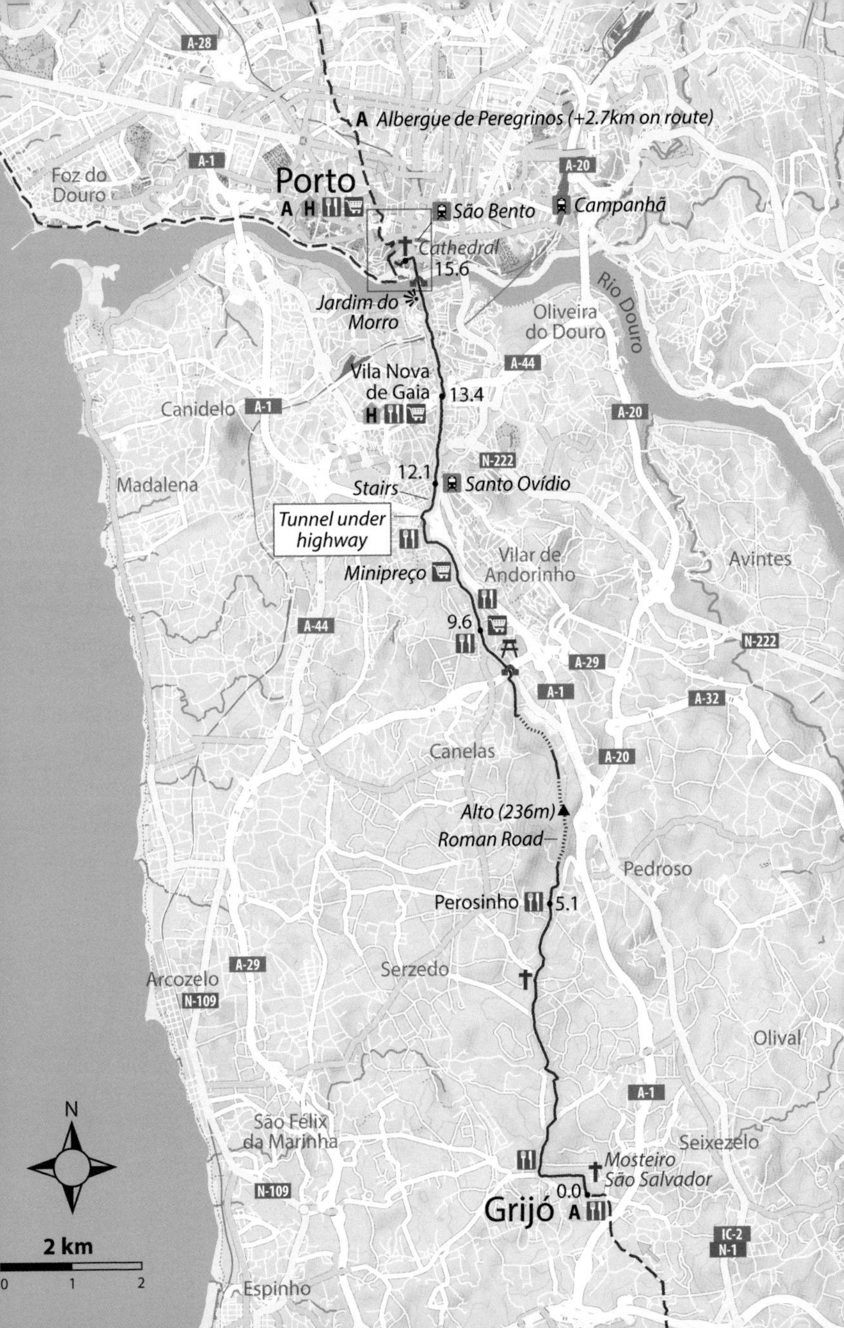

A-28
A Albergue de Peregrinos (+2.7km on route)
A-1
A-20
Foz do Douro
Porto
São Bento
Campanhã
Cathedral
15.6
Rio Douro
Jardim do Morro
Oliveira do Douro
A-44
Vila Nova de Gaia
13.4
Canidelo
A-1
A-20
N-222
12.1
Santo Ovídio
Madalena
Stairs
Tunnel under highway
Vilar de Andorinho
Avintes
Minipreço
9.6
A-44
N-222
A-29
A-1
A-32
Canelas
A-20
Alto (236m)
Roman Road
Pedroso
Perosinho
5.1
Serzedo
A-29
Arcozelo
N-109
Olival
A-1
N
São Félix da Marinha
Seixezelo
Mosteiro São Salvador
0.0
N-109
Grijó
IC-2
N-1
2 km
0
1
2
Espinho

Porto
7 ViaPortuscale (near Senhora da Hora metro station)
1 Albergue de Peregrinos (on-route, 2.7km from cathedral)
13 República
City Drops 12
Trindade (Metro)
Spot 11
Portuense 21
Del Norte 20
Central and Coastal Routes (Official)
6 Gallery
18 Lusitana
5 Invictus
Praça de Carlos Alberto
Jardim da Carregal
Aliados (Metro)
Sport 10
(near near metro stations Campanha and 24 de Agosto)
Vivacity 17
4 Downtown
8 N.S. do Rosário
Igreja do Carmo
16 França
Porto University
Livraria Lello
Bonfim 9
Belo Sonho 19
Peninsular 15
Praça da Liberdade
Praça de Lisboa
São Bento (Train)
Jardim da Cordoaria
Torre dos Clérigos
3 Yes!
Laventura
São Bento (Metro)
Parque do Horto das Virtudes
14 Poets
Turn L, going up Rua do Ferraz
Misericórdia
Sé Cathedral
Museu de Arte Sacre
2 Bluesock
São Francisco
São Nicolau
Praça Ribeira
Senda Litoral
Douro
100m
N
Breiner
Cedofeita
Mirante
Mártires da Liberdade
Almada
Alferes Malheiro
Dr. Ricardo Jorge
Miguel Bombarda
Praça do Município
José Falcão
Túnel
Carmo
Prof. Vicente José de Carvalho
Restauração
Carmelitas
Mártires da Pátria
Clérigos
R. Campo dos
R. dos Caldeireiros
Aliados
Ferraz
Flores
São Bento da Vitória
Vitória
Dom Afonso Henriques
Silva
Belomonte
Nova da Alfândega
Ferreira Borges
Mouzinho da
Comércio do Porto
Bolsa
Infante D. Henrique
Cais da Ribeira

Route Options: Porto to Redondela

From Porto, the Camino splits into two main alternative routes, the Central and Coastal, which reconvene in Redondela, Spain (6-7 stages). In the first two stages, there are waymarked paths connecting the two routes.

Central Route: (6 stages, 161.0km): Historical traditional pilgrim route, more albergues and walkers, hillier, village to village feel, more established, less likely to undergo route changes
Coastal Route (7 stages, 186.3km): Gaining in popularity, coastal views, feels somewhat touristy in beach areas, less developed and less formal

❶ Central Route: Stages 16-22

The Central Route continues north from Porto through the densely populated Porto metro area. Services are plentiful, especially for the first 10km. The route is well waymarked and relatively easy to follow. To avoid urban walking, taking the metro to Vilar de Pinheiro stop saves 18km. (From there you could walk to São Pedro de Rates [~20km] and to Portela de Tamal [~27km] the following day). If you want to walk the Central Route but would still like a taste of the coast while avoiding some of Porto's urban sprawl, you can walk the coast to Vila do Conde (see route option 2b), before following a waymarked connecting to Arcos.

2a Coastal Route (Official): Stages 16a-23a

The official Coastal Route leaves Porto the same as the Central Route. The routes split at a roadside cross 6.8km after the cathedral. The Coastal Route turns L on Rua do Senhor and then continues on Rua da Fonte Velha, while the Central Route continues straight. This route then leads to Vila do Conde entirely on hard surfaces, passing the Porto Airport. As this first day is all urban pavement, the Senda Litoral alternate Coastal Route is highly recommended, and you can continue on the official route from Vila do Conde.

2b Coastal Route (Senda Litoral): Stage 16a

Follows the Douro River and Atlantic coastline to Vila do Conde; from before Foz do Douro largely following pedestrian/cycle ways that alternate between pavement and boardwalk. This route feels touristy, but pleasant. While poorly marked, navigation along the river and coastline is fairly straightforward. From the cathedral (Sé do Porto), descend to Praça da Ribeira along Rua de São João; from there follow the river west, soon joining the main road (Rua Nova da Alfândega) and passing the Museu do Transportes and Museo do Vinho do Porto on your way out of town. Later, leaving Vila Chá, waymarks suggest returning inland, but it's best to continue along the coast. (Marks along the coast later reappear and guide you the final few kilometers into Vila do Conde.) You can also easily shave distance from this route (11.7km) by taking the metro to Matosinhos. Alternatively, you can stop in Angeiras (Orbitur Camping offers pilgrim rates in bungalows), Labruge (very pleasant municipal albergue), or Vila Chã. Both Coastal routes rejoin just before crossing the bridge into Vila do Conde.

It is possible to continue following the coastline north after this stage, but this route is not consistently waymarked and requires route finding and flexibility. We do not detail the Senda Litoral on maps after 16a, though there are 💡 tips that point out some sections that are nice.

16 PORTO TO VILARINHO

27.3km (17.0mi), 7-9.5 Hours, Difficulty:
P 98%, 26.8km, U 2%, 0.5km

See previous page for route options leaving Porto. Many pilgrims start from Porto, making the Camino busier going forward. See p. 78 for Coastal Routes maps and route information.

17.5 Vilar de Pinheiro

H Residencial Santa Marinha (€20/25): wifi, José Régio 1330, 229271520, +500m

22.6 Gião

H Casa Mindela (€57-100): wifi, Joudina 427, 914118018, +500m on N-306

25.7 Vairão

A Mosteiro de Vairão (par, 80, €5): Convento 21, 252662100, +200m

27.3 Vilarinho

1. **A H Casa Família Vidal** (6, €10/-/20): wifi, Salteiro 87, 252661503
2. **A H Casa da Laura** (6, €12/-/30): wifi, Estreita 112, 917767307

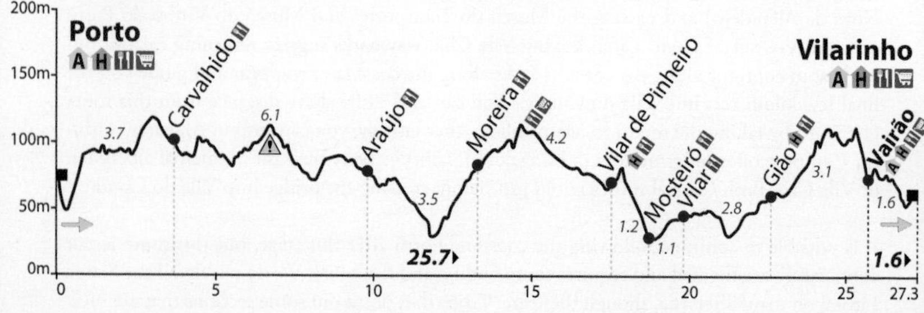

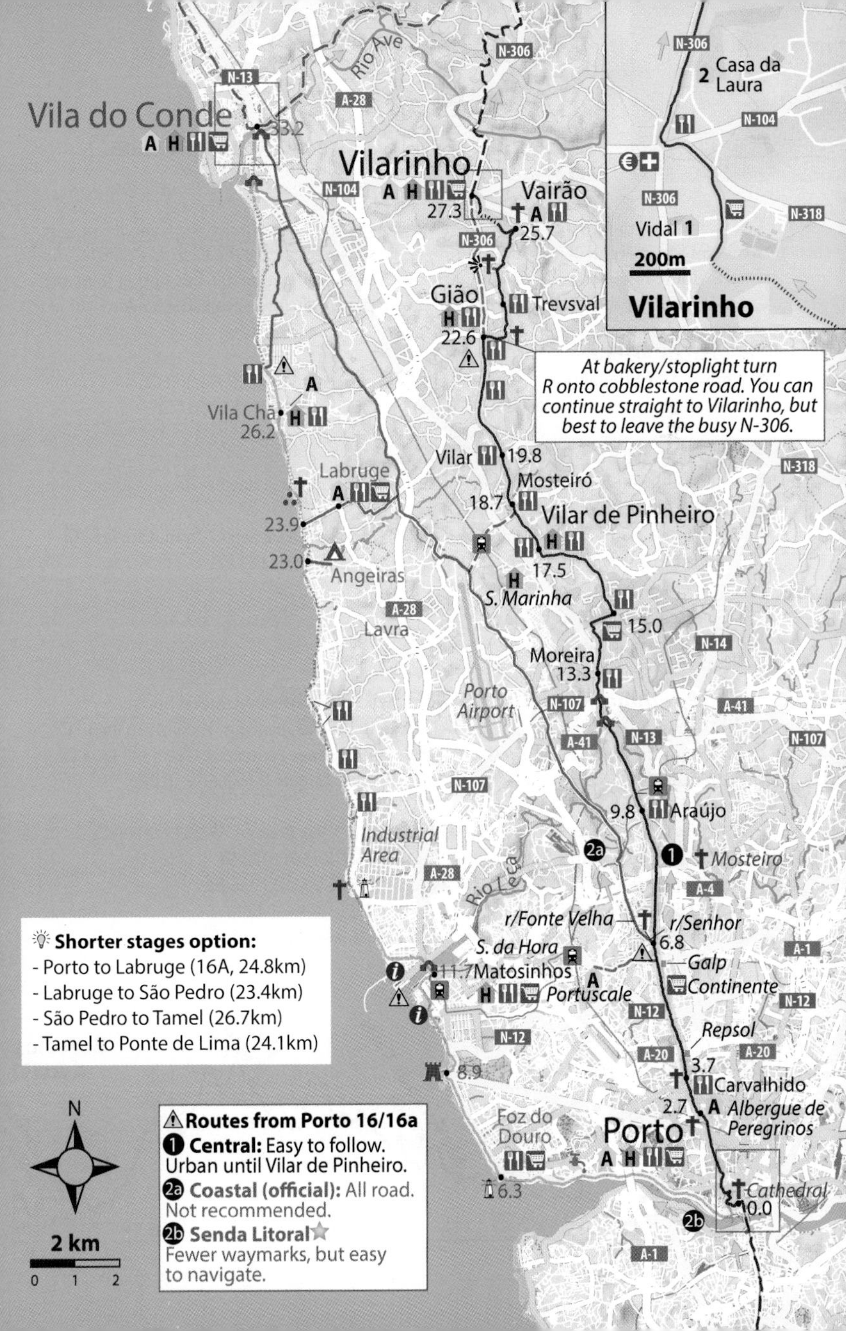

Vila do Conde
33.2
Vilarinho
27.3
Vairão
25.7
Gião
22.6
Trevsval
At bakery/stoplight turn R onto cobblestone road. You can continue straight to Vilarinho, but best to leave the busy N-306.
Vila Chã
26.2
Labruge
23.9
23.0
Angeiras
Vilar
19.8
Mosteiró
18.7
Vilar de Pinheiro
17.5
S. Marinha
15.0
Lavra
Moreira
13.3
Porto Airport
Rio Ave
Rio Leça
Industrial Area
9.8
Araújo
Mosteiro
r/Fonte Velha
r/Senhor
6.8
S. da Hora
Galp
11.7 Matosinhos
Portuscale
Continente
Repsol
3.7
8.9
Carvalhido
2.7
Albergue de Peregrinos
Foz do Douro
Porto
6.3
Cathedral
0.0
Casa da Laura
Vidal
200m
Vilarinho
N-13
N-306
N-104
N-318
N-14
N-107
N-12
A-28
A-41
A-4
A-1
A-20
Shorter stages option:
- Porto to Labruge (16A, 24.8km)
- Labruge to São Pedro (23.4km)
- São Pedro to Tamel (26.7km)
- Tamel to Ponte de Lima (24.1km)
Routes from Porto 16/16a
1 Central: Easy to follow. Urban until Vilar de Pinheiro.
2a Coastal (official): All road. Not recommended.
2b Senda Litoral Fewer waymarks, but easy to navigate.
N
2 km
0 1 2

17 VILARINHO TO BARCELOS

29.1km (18.1mi), 8-10 Hours, Difficulty:
P 81%, 23.5km, U 19%, 5.6km

If you walked the Coastal Route to Vila do Conde, you can return to the Central Route at Arcos and São Pedro de Rates. At São Pedro de Rates, you can leave the Central Route for the Coastal Route by following a marked dirt track (an old railroad bed). This option joins the Coastal Route in Fão. If you're planning to stay in private albergues, consider booking ahead.

8.2 Arcos

H **Quinta São Miguel** (€60+): , Igreja 209, 919372202
H **Villa d'Arcos** (€60-80): , Alegria 38, 252652041, 965853567

12.1 São Pedro de Rates

Popular albergue and ideal stopping point to shorten the next day by 10km walking from São Pedro to Tamel (26.7km).
A **S. Pedro de Rates** (assoc, 50, don): , 2-10pm, Mar-Sep (2-9pm, Oct-Feb)
H **Casa Mattos** (€40): , Direita 240, 919822398, 916005172

20.0 Pedra Furada

A H **Pedra Furada** (5, €10/-/25): , 252951144

28.1 Barcelinhos/Barcelos

Medieval bridge.

1. A **Amigos da Montanha** (assoc, 16, €5): , Penedos 39, 253830430
2. A **Senhor do Galo** (assoc, 40, €5): , Guil. Gomes Fernandes, 253833304
3. A **Cidade de Barcelos** (muni, 26, don): , Miguel Bombarda 36 , key: Café Araújo
4. H **BWay** (€35-50): , Custódio José Gomes Vilas Boas 44, 253825090
5. H **Residencial Arantes** (€20-30/30-45): , 253811326
6. H **Bagoeira** (€45-55): , Dr. Sidónio Pais 495, 253811236
7. H **Hotel do Terço** (€45-55): , São Bento 7, 253808380
8. H **Dom Nuno** (€56/74): , D. Nuno Alvares Pereira 90, 269823325

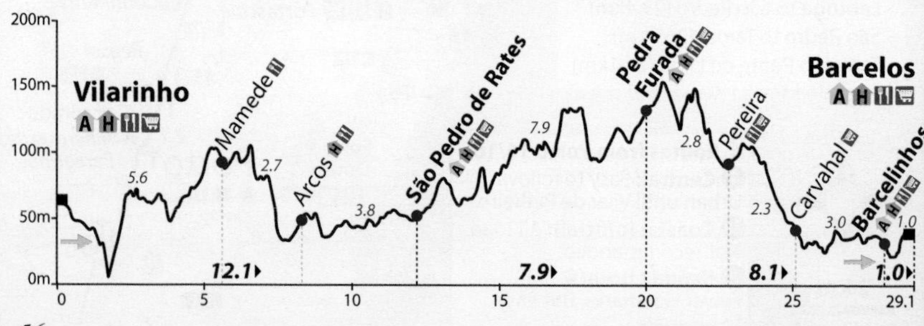

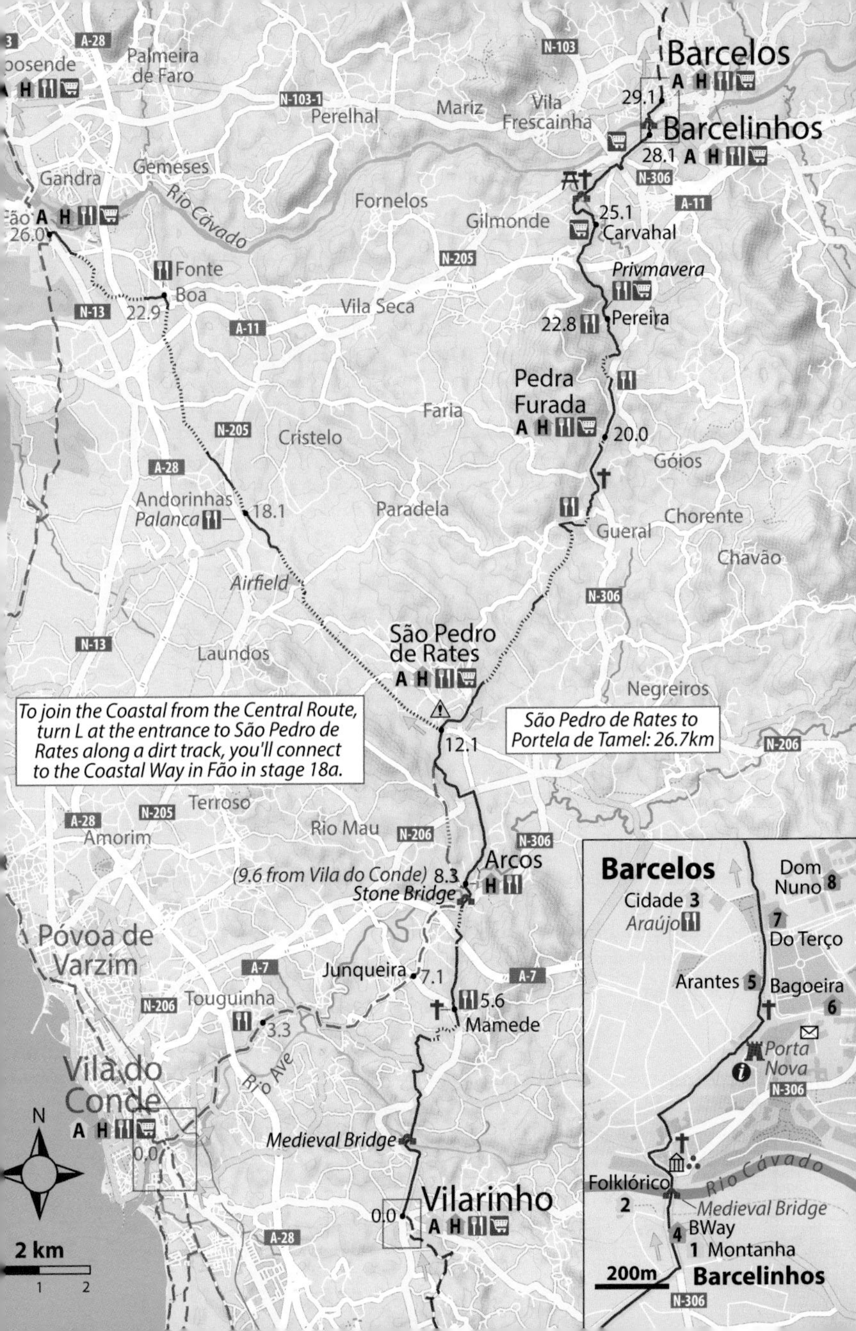

Barcelos
29.1
Barcelinhos
28.1
Palmeira de Faro
Perelhal
Mariz
Vila Frescainha
Gemeses
Gandra
Rio Cávado
Fornelos
Gilmonde
25.1
Carvahal
Fão
26.0
Fonte Boa
22.9
Vila Seca
Privmavera
22.8
Pereira
Pedra Furada
20.0
Faria
Cristelo
Góios
Andorinhas
Palanca
18.1
Paradela
Chorente
Gueral
Chavão
Airfield
São Pedro de Rates
Laundos
Negreiros
To join the Coastal from the Central Route, turn L at the entrance to São Pedro de Rates along a dirt track, you'll connect to the Coastal Way in Fão in stage 18a.
12.1
São Pedro de Rates to Portela de Tamel: 26.7km
Terroso
Rio Mau
Amorim
Arcos
(9.6 from Vila do Conde) 8.3
Stone Bridge
Póvoa de Varzim
Junqueira
7.1
Touguinha
3.3
5.6
Mamede
Rio Ave
Vila do Conde
0.0
Medieval Bridge
Vilarinho
0.0
N
2 km
1
2
A-28
N-103
N-103-1
N-306
A-11
N-205
N-13
N-206
A-7
Barcelos
Dom Nuno 8
Cidade 3
Araújo
7 Do Terço
Arantes 5
Bagoeira 6
Porta Nova
Rio Cávado
Folklórico
2
Medieval Bridge
4 BWay
1 Montanha
200m
Barcelinhos

18 BARCELOS TO PONTE DE LIMA

33.8km (21.0mi), **9.5-12 Hours, Difficulty:**
P 81%, 27.5km, U 19%, 6.3km

One of the longest stages of the entire route, but one with many intermediate lodging options. Stopping in Lugar do Corgo (at ★Casa da Fernanda) or Vitarino dos Piães affords a short following day to Ponte de Lima or a longer, challenging day to Rubiães. There are relatively few beds at private, intermediate accommodations—best to reserve in advance.

9.8 **Tamel São Pedro Fins** A A pleasant hilltop location. No stores, but the albergue sells basic supplies and a delivery truck selling bread comes to the albergue every evening. Restaurant 2000 is across from the albergue. Train station is 1.7km past the albergue.
A **Recoleta** (muni, 42, €5): Recoleta 100, 253137075, 3pm a.y.

15.4 **Balugães** H The route skirts Balugães; most services are off-route.
H **Quinta da Cancela** (€65/80): C. Batista de Sousa 275, 258763079
H **Casas do Rio** (€55-87/65-97): Navió 75, 969312585, +1.2km

19.7 **Lugar do Corgo** A
A ★ **Casa da Fernanda** (14, don): 914589521, family-run, communal meals

22.0 **Vitarino dos Piães** A H
A **Casa Sagres** (6, €15): Latão 175, 962916441, after church
H **Estábulo Valinhas** (€35+): Fonte Quente 251, 961050955

24.4 **Facha** A H
A H **Quinta da Portela** (6, €15/-/70): 964257171, call in advance

28.0 **Seara** H
H **Residencial Pinheiro Manso** (€45+): Travessa do Craston 15, 258943775

33.8 **Ponte de Lima** A H
Accommodations under city map on opposite page.

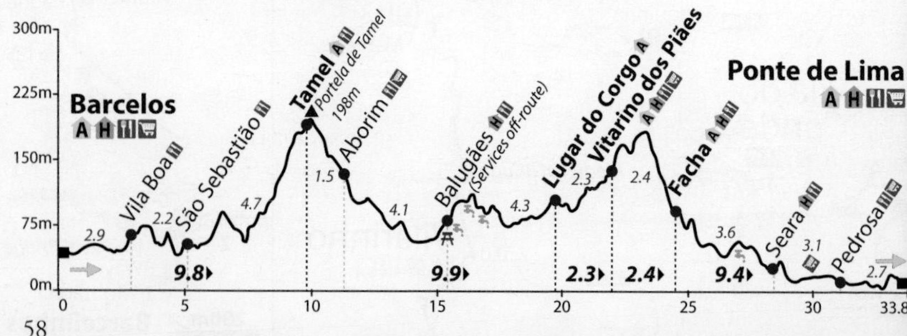

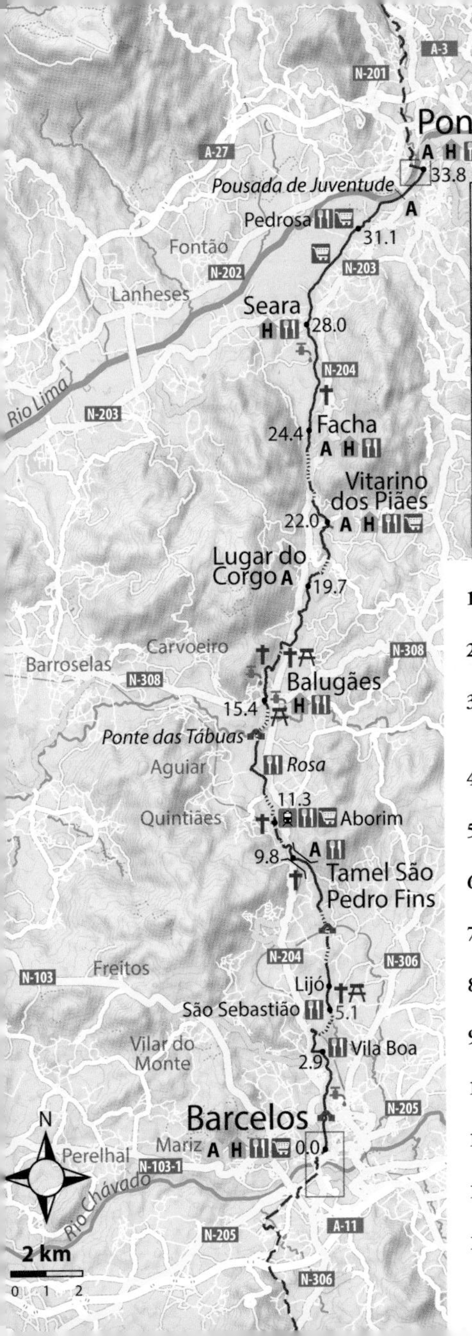

A-3
N-201
N-202
IC-28
N-203
Ponte de Lima
A H
A-27
33.8
Pousada de Juventude
A
Pedrosa
31.1
Fontão
N-202
N-203
Lanheses
Seara
H
28.0
N-204
Rio Lima
N-203
24.4
Facha
A H
Vitarino
dos Piães
22.0
A H
Lugar do
Corgo A
19.7
Carvoeiro
N-308
Barroselas
N-308
Balugães
15.4
H
Ponte das Tábuas
Aguiar
Rosa
11.3
Quintiães
Aborim
A
9.8
Tamel São
Pedro Fins
N-204
N-306
N-103
Freitos
Lijó
São Sebastião
5.1
Vilar do
Monte
Vila Boa
2.9
N-205
Barcelos
N
Mariz
A H
0.0
Perelhal
N-103-1
Rio Chávado
A-11
N-205
2 km
N-306
0 1 2

Arc'otel
12 1 Municipal
13
Arrabalde
São
João 10
11
Casa da Vila
Ponte
de Lima
Medieval
Bridge
9 Beira Rio
8 Mercearia
da Vila
Rio Lima
6 Encanada
200m
5 Império
do Norte
7 Pinheiro
Old Village 3
InLima 4
2
Juventude

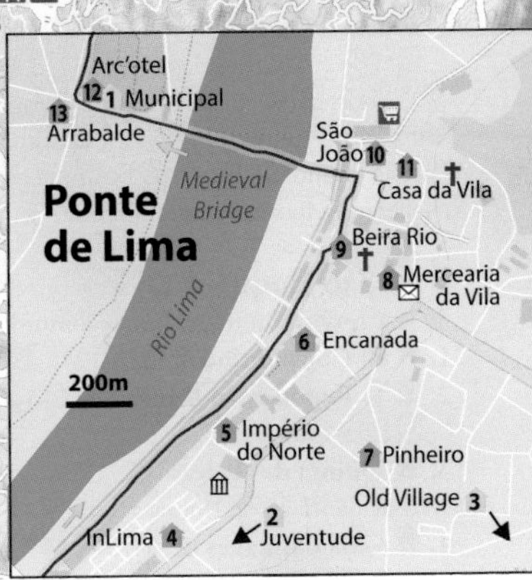

1. **A Municipal** (60, €5): , Largo da Alegria, 925403164, 4pm, Apr-Oct
2. **A H P. de Juventude** (60, €13/-/32): , P. João Paulo II, 258751321
3. **A H Old Village** (20, €18/-/40): , Foral Velho de D. Teresa 1415, 961574929
4. **H InLima** (€60): , Agostinho José Taveira, Lote 6, 258900050
5. **H Império do Norte** (€50/55-60): , 5 de Outubro 97, 258009008
6. **H Encanada** (€35/40): , 25 de Abril 30, 258941189
7. **H Casa do Pinheiro** (€55/65-70): , Gen. Norton de Matos 629, 258943971
8. **H Mercearia da Vila** (€65-80): , Cardeal Saraiva 34-36, 258753562
9. **H Beira Rio** (€35): , 25 de Abril 11, 258944044
10. **H São João** (€25/35): , São João 44, 258941288
11. **H Casa da Vila** (€50): , Beato Francisco Pacheco 23, 962965359
12. **H Arc'otel** (€60+): , Alegria 9, 258900150
13. **H Casa do Arrabalde** (€65/80): , Dr. Francisco Abreu Maia, 258742442

19

PONTE DE LIMA TO RUBIÃES

18.3km (11.4mi), 5-7 Hours, Difficulty:

P 45%, 8.3km, U 55%, 10.0km

A shorter day that continues through hilly, rural countryside on cobblestone roads and dirt paths. Wonderful views await at the top of a long climb to the day's high point at Alto de Portela Grande (400m). ⚠ Both the ascent and descent are quite rocky and can be especially challenging in wet weather—you'll be glad for trekking poles today.

16.7 São Roque A H

Few services in town, but accommodations offer shuttle services to nearby restaurants.

1. A H **Constantino** (€12/12/24): , São Pedro de Rubiães, 251782390
2. H **O Repouso do Peregrino** (€15+/30): , S. Pedro de Rubiães 2192, 251943692
3. H **Quinta das Leiras** (€29-35/48-54): , C. de Santiago de Rubiães 576, +491743239436
4. H **Casa das Lages** (€15+/30): , Caminho de Santiago 550, 964936366

18.3 Rubiães A H

A café across from the municipal albergue sells snacks. Restaurant Bom Retiro has a nice pilgrim menu. There is a small grocery store where N-201 crosses the Coura River.

1. A **Municipal** (48, €5): , N201 344, 917164476, all year
2. A H **Casa São Sebastião** (4, €15/-/30): , N201 346, 968998802
3. A ☆ **O Ninho** (17, €12): , 251941002, 200m past the municipal albergue on N-201; very cozy

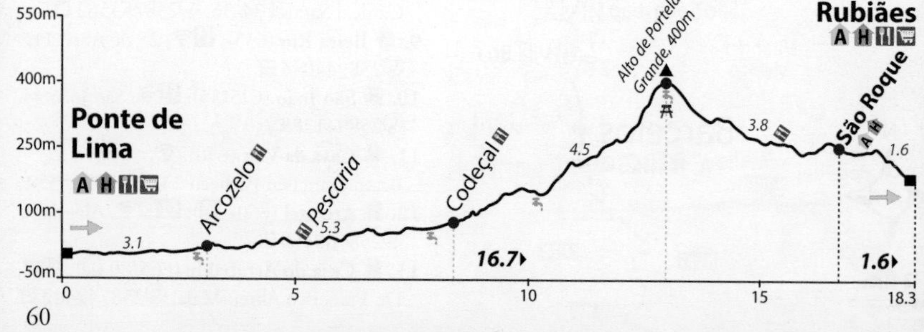

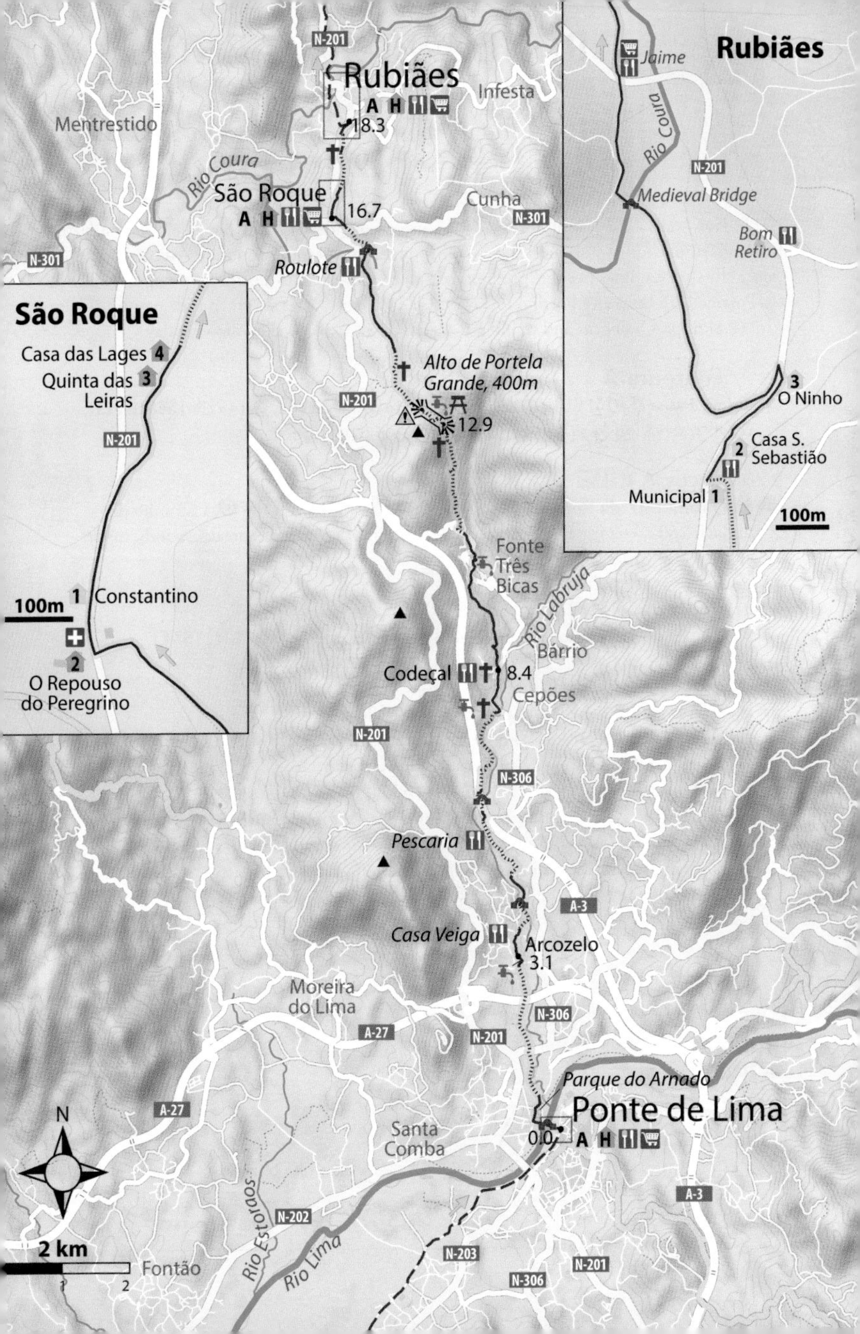

Rubiães
A H
18.3
Infesta
Mentrestido
Rio Coura
São Roque
A H
16.7
Cunha
N-201
N-301
Roulote
Alto de Portela
Grande, 400m
12.9
Fonte
Três
Bicas
Rio Labruja
Bárrio
Codeçal
8.4
Cepões
N-306
Pescaria
A-3
Casa Veiga
Arcozelo
3.1
Moreira
do Lima
A-27
Parque do Arnado
Ponte de Lima
0.0
A H
Santa
Comba
N-202
N-203
Rio Estoraos
Rio Lima
Fontão
2 km
N
São Roque
Casa das Lages 4
Quinta das 3
Leiras
100m
1 Constantino
2
O Repouso
do Peregrino
Rubiães
Jaime
Medieval Bridge
Bom
Retiro
3
O Ninho
2 Casa S.
Sebastião
Municipal 1
100m

20 RUBIÃES TO VALENÇA

16.7km (10.4mi), 4-5.5 Hours, Difficulty:
P 75%, 12.6km, U 25%, 4.1km

Today's walk—the last in Portugal—begins as a wonderful stroll along cobblestone paths through rural countryside and villages with stunning flowers in springtime. Approaching Valença the surroundings become progressively more congested. If the next two stages—Valença to Porriño (20.3km) and Porriño to Redondela (15.5km)—feel short, consider continuing to Tui (2.8km past Valença) and walking to Redondela (33.0km) the following day.

7.3 Fontoura A

A **Pilger Pause** (14, €13): São Miguel 1161, +491781848141, accepts reservations, call between 11am and 1pm to confirm

9.5 Paços A H

A H **Quinta Estrada Romana** (12, €25/-/60): Caminho de Santiago 1607, 251837333, all year, dorm price includes breakfast and dinner; call ahead in winter

10.6 Pedreira A H

A H **Quinta do Caminho** (28, €10/-/65): 251821183

16.7 Valença A H

Interesting walled medieval city with impressive fortress

1. A **Albergue São Teotónio** (85, €5): 251821183, 926002045
2. H **Residencial São Gião** (€20/25+): São Teotónio 17, 251030040
3. H **Val Flores** (€25+/35+): Bombeiros Voluntários 12, 251824106
4. H **Lara** (€40/55): Bombeiros Voluntários, 251824348
5. H **Portas do Sol** (€25+/35-40): Conselheiro Lopes da Silva 51, 965851667
6. H **Pousada de São Teotónio** (-/€95+): Baluarte do Socorro, 251800260
7. H **Casa do Poço** (-/€100): Calçada da Gaviarra 4, 251010094, 912979373

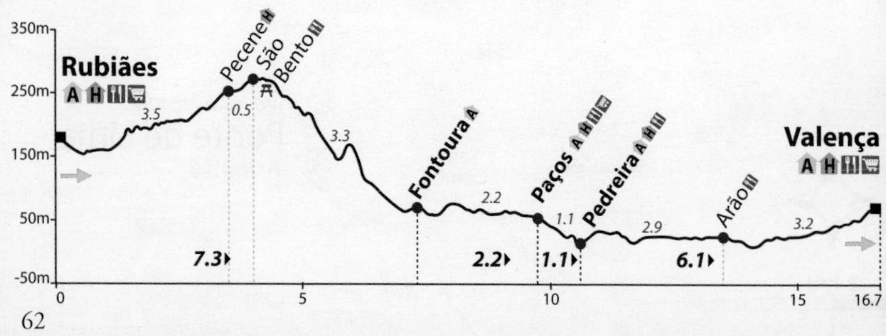

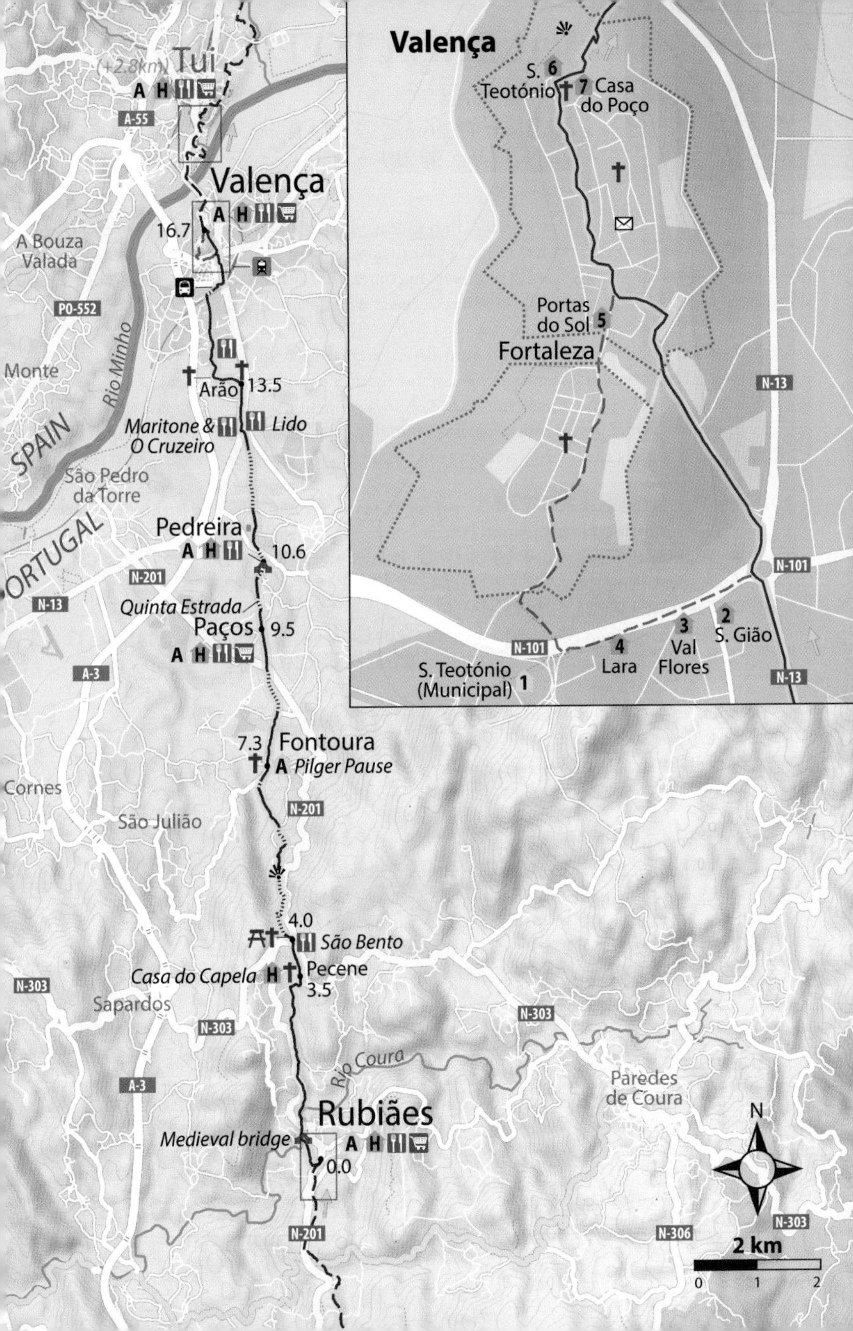

Valença
S. Teotónio 6
7 Casa do Poço
Portas do Sol 5
Fortaleza
N-13
N-101
N-101
2 S. Gião
3 Val Flores
4 Lara
S. Teotónio (Municipal) 1
N-13
(+2.8km) Tui
A H
A-55
Valença
A H
16.7
A Bouza Valada
PO-552
Rio Minho
Monte
Arão 13.5
Maritone & O Cruzeiro
Lido
SPAIN
São Pedro da Torre
ORTUGAL
Pedreira
A H
10.6
N-201
N-13
Quinta Estrada
Paços
9.5
A H
A-3
7.3
Fontoura
A Pilger Pause
Cornes
N-201
São Julião
4.0
São Bento
Casa do Capela H
Pecene
3.5
N-303
Sapardos
N-303
N-303
Rio Coura
Paredes de Coura
A-3
Rubiães
Medieval bridge
A H
0.0
N
N-201
N-306
N-303
2 km
0
1
2

21 VALENÇA TO PORRIÑO

20.3km (12.6mi), 5-6.5 Hours, Difficulty:

67%, 13.6km, 33%, 6.7km

Start by crossing the Rio Minho/Miño to leave Portugal and enter Spain. Remember to turn your watch ahead one hour (3pm in Portugal is 4pm in Spain) and use Spain's country code (+34) when calling Spanish numbers. In contrast to Portugal, Spanish grocery stores are likely to be closed Sundays; take this into account when planning your meals.

Pleasant walking day near the Louro River, alternating between dirt paths, cobblestone roads, and pavement. 11.5km into the day, shortly after reaching a paved road where you pass several large roadside paintings, you reach a ⚠ tricky junction where many marks have clearly been erased. While some marks suggest continuing straight, it's best to turn L onto a dirt road, soon crossing the Louro River (and once again finding marks that have escaped erasure).

2.8 **Tui** A H Tui offers many accommodations—consider walking from Rubiães to Tui. If walking past Porriño, there are several albergues in the next 12km.

1. A **Municipal** (48, €6): , Párroco Rodríguez Vázquez 0, 638276685
2. A H **Ideas Peregrinas** (17, €13): , Porta da Pía 1, 986076330
3. A **Tui Hostel** (24, €12): , Bispo Lago 5, 986627979
4. A **Santo Domingo** (14, €12-15): , Antero Rubin 20, 650820685
5. A H **San Clemente** (23, €12/25/35): , Canónigo Valiño 23, 678747700
6. H **O Novo Cabalo Furado** (€50): , Seijas 3, 986604445, 640547601
7. H **A Torre do Xudeu** (€40/60): , Tide 3, 986603535
8. H **Villa Blanca** (€40/50+): , Augusto González Besada 5, 986603525
9. H **Colón** (€45/55): , Colón 11, 986600223

20.3 **Porriño** A H

1. A **Municipal** (52, €6): , Buenos Aires 17, 986335428
2. A **Camino Portugués** (52, €10-12): , Buenos Aires 40, 886133252
3. H **Hostal Louro** (€23/34): , Buenos Aires 6, 986330048
4. H **Parque** (€30/45): , Servando Ramilo 6, 986331504
5. H **Azul** (€40): , Ramirás 38, 986330032, 986330176

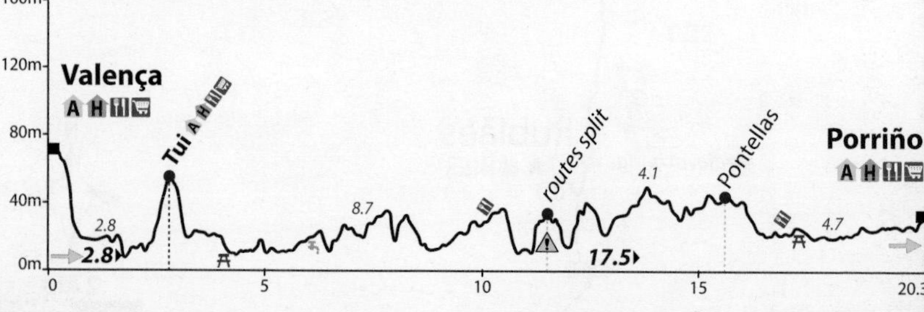

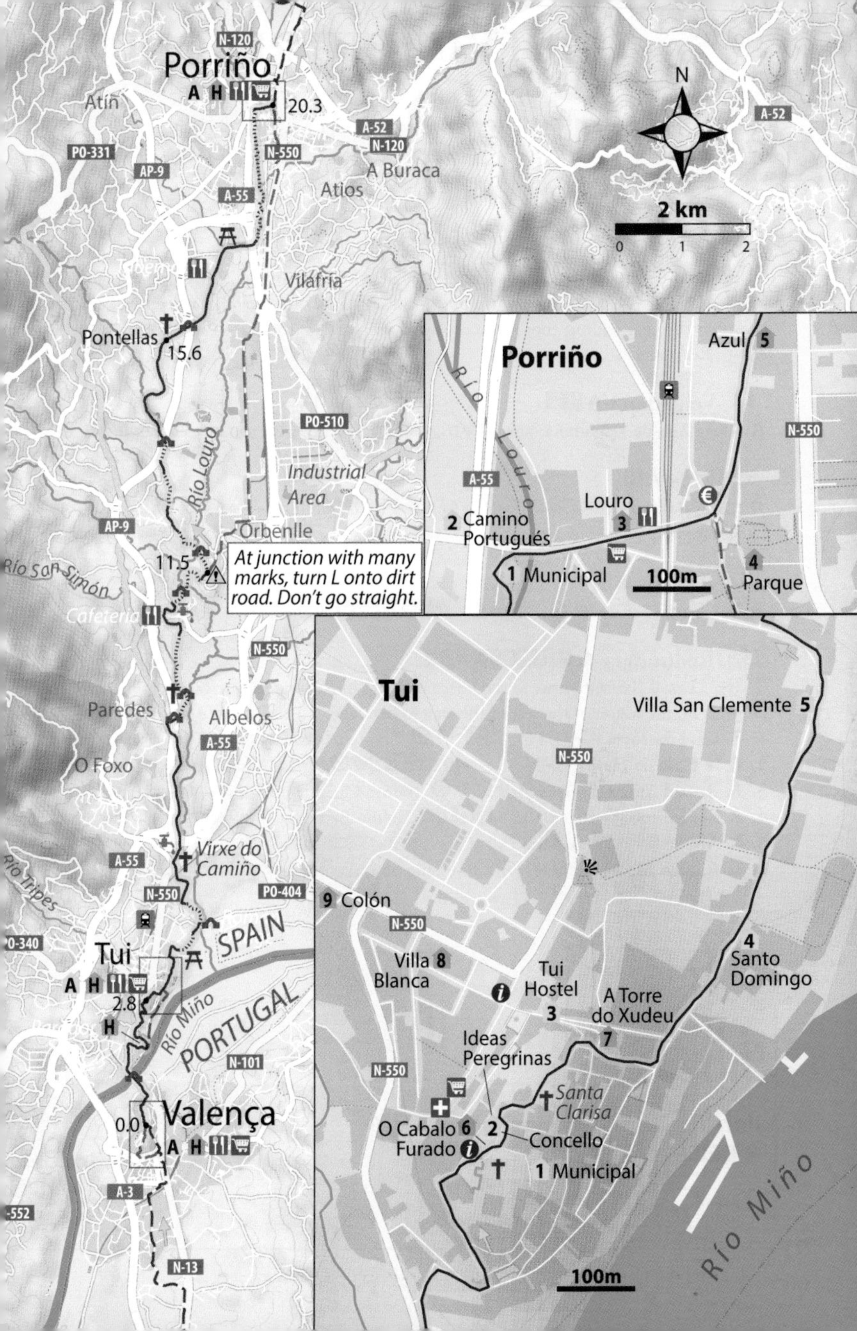

Porriño
A H
20.3
Atín
N-120
A-52
PO-331
AP-9
N-550
A Buraca
Atios
A-55
Vilafría
Pontellas
15.6
PO-510
Río Louro
Industrial Area
Orbenlle
11.5
At junction with many marks, turn L onto dirt road. Don't go straight.
Río San Simón
Cafetería
Paredes
Albelos
O Foxo
Virxe do Camiño
PO-404
SPAIN
Tui
A H
2.8
H
Río Miño
PORTUGAL
N-101
Valença
0.0
A H
A-3
N-13
2 km
0 1 2
N
Porriño
Río Louro
Azul 5
Louro 3
2 Camino Portugués
1 Municipal
4 Parque
100m
Tui
Villa San Clemente 5
9 Colón
Villa 8 Blanca
Tui Hostel 3
A Torre do Xudeu 7
4 Santo Domingo
Ideas Peregrinas
Santa Clarisa
O Cabalo 6 Furado
2 Concello
1 Municipal
Río Miño
100m

22 PORRIÑO TO REDONDELA

15.5km (9.6mi), 4-5 Hours, Difficulty:
88%, 13.7km, 12%, 1.8km

Leaving Porriño, the built-up business and residential area proves a bit of a slog, but soon the walk becomes more enjoyable passing through Veigadaña and Mos and climbing to the Santiaguiño de Anta Chapel. Two kilometers after Vilar de Infesta, there's a perfect picnic spot (complete with picnic tables) in a pine forest. After lunch, enjoy the views as you descend (steeply!) through Padrón (not to be confused with the larger Padrón in stage 25) on your way to Redondela.

3.2 Veigadaña A

A **Santa Ana de Veigadaña** (assoc, 16, €7): , Cam. das Lagoas 6, 986094277

5.9 Mos A

A **Santa Baias de Mos** (assoc, 16, €6): , Camiño da Rua 3, 986348001, register and pay in Café Flora

12.1 Padrón A

A **Bar Corisco** (12, €10-15/25/30): , Romano 47, 986402166

15.5 Redondela A H

The Coastal Route returns to the Central Route in Redondela, increasing the number of pilgrims on the route for the rest of the way to Santiago.

1. A **Casa da Torre** (34, €6): , Praza de Ribadavia, 986404196,
2. A H **Casa da Herba** (24, €12/-/40): , Pr. da Alfóndiga, 644404074
3. A **Rosa d'Abreu** (6, €15): , Isidoro Queimaliños 33, 688422701
4. A **El Camino** (40, €10-12): , Telmo Bernadez 11, 650963676
5. H **Alvear** (€40+/50+): , Pai Crespo 30, 986400637
6. H **Rua do Medio** (€20/38): , Reveriano Soutullo 46, 666764908

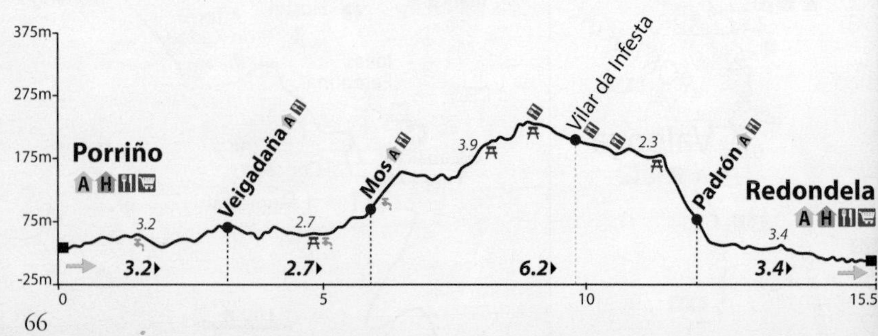

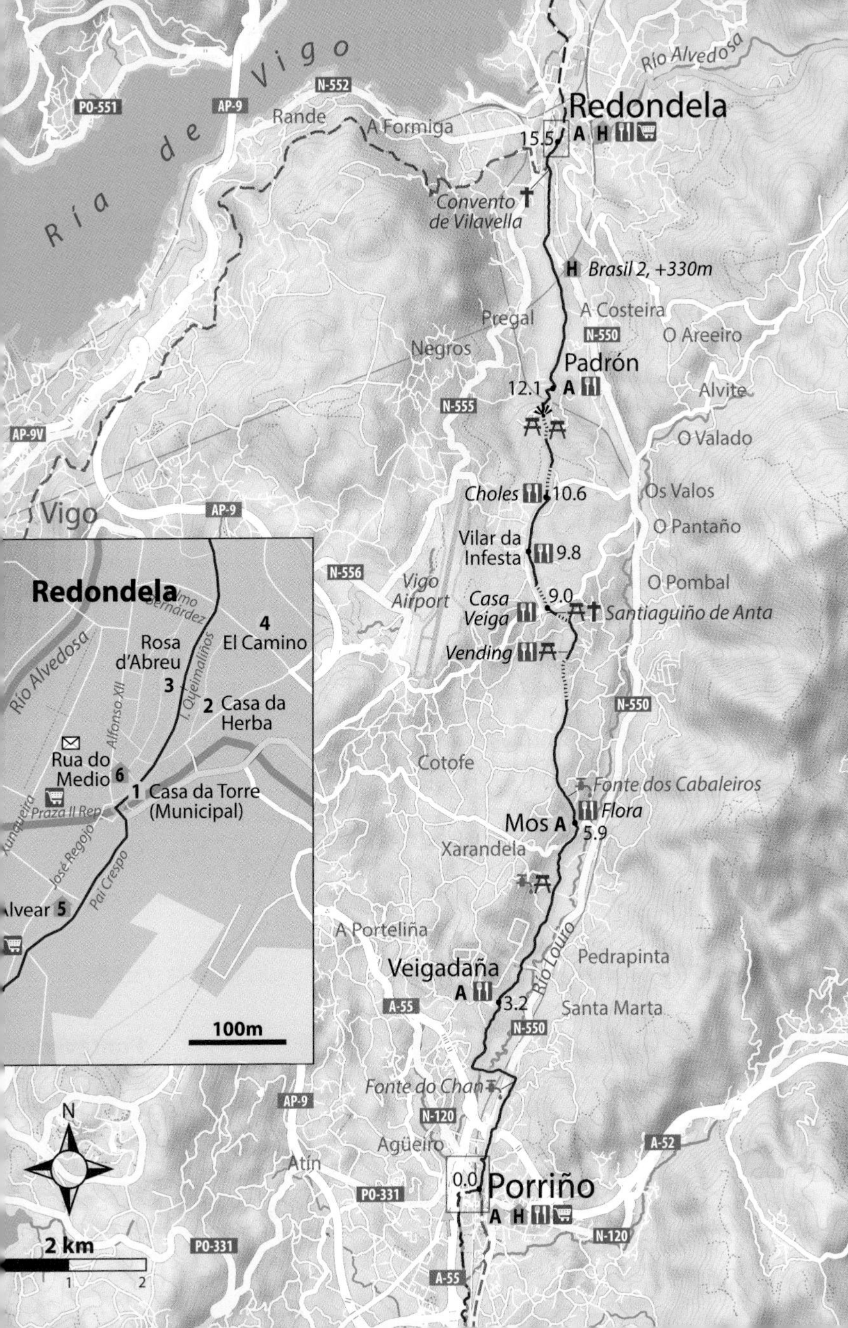
Ría de Vigo
Redondela
A H
15.5
Rande
A Formiga
Río Alvedosa
N-552
PO-551
AP-9
Convento de Vilavella
Brasil 2, +330m
A Costeira
Pregal
N-550
O Areeiro
Negros
Padrón
12.1
A
Alvite
N-555
O Valado
AP-9V
Choles
10.6
Os Valos
Vigo
AP-9
O Pantaño
Vilar da Infesta
9.8
N-556
O Pombal
Vigo Airport
Casa Veiga
9.0
Santiaguiño de Anta
Vending
N-550
Cotofe
Fonte dos Cabaleiros
Flora
Mos A
5.9
Xarandela
A Porteliña
Pedrapinta
Río Louro
Veigadaña
A
3.2
Santa Marta
A-55
N-550
Fonte do Chan
AP-9
N-120
Agüeiro
A-52
Atín
0.0
Porriño
A H
PO-331
N-120
PO-331
A-55
N
2 km
1
2
Redondela
Río Alvedosa
4 El Camino
Rosa d'Abreu
3
2 Casa da Herba
Alfonso XII
I. Queimaliños
Rua do Medio 6
1 Casa da Torre (Municipal)
Praza II Rep.
José Regojo
Pai Crespo
Alvear 5
100m

23 REDONDELA TO PONTEVEDRA

19.7km (12.2mi), 5.5-7 HOURS, DIFFICULTY:

P 72%, 14.3km, U 28%, 5.5km

Enjoy countryside with many picnic spots, especially after Arcade. Watch the L turn to a cobblestone alley after Ponte Sampaio. You can detour along the Río Tomeza into Pontevedra.

3.1 Cesantes A H

Cesantes is off-route to the west, but accommodations are to the L and R when you reach highway N-550, 3.1km past Redondela.

A H **Pensión Jumboli** (12, €10/-/35+): , Carballiño 9, 986495066

A H **O Refuxio de la Jerezana** (12, €12/15/30): , Pereiro 43, 601165977, Mar-Sep, prices listed for pilgrims with credencial

7.6 Arcade A H

A **O Recuncho do Peregrino** (29, €10): , Soutoxuste 45, 617292598, 2pm Jan-Oct, L on N-550, 2km before Arcade, +300m

A **Lameiriñas** (29, €12): , Lameiriñas 8, 616107820, Mar-Oct

A H **O Lar de Pepa** (18, €10/-/20): , Ribeiro 1, 986678006, quaint, fun

H **Durate** (€25/40): , Lameiriñas 8, 986670057

H **Avenida** (€24/36-40): , Rodrigo A. Castelao 1, 986670100

19.7 Pontevedra A H

1. A **La Virgen Peregrina** (muni, 56, €6): , Ramón Otero Pedraio, 986844045, 1pm-10pm, a.y., southern edge of town, adjacent to train station
2. A **Aloxa** (59, €14): , Gorgullón 68, 986896453, noon, Apr-O.
3. A H **Slow City Hostel** (€18/-/40): , Amargura 5, 631062896
4. H **Resid. Peregrino** (€40+): , Ramón Otero Pedrayo 8, 986858409
5. H **La Peregrina** (€33/48): , Eduardo Pondal 76, 986850145, 986866249
6. H **Avenida** (€32+/45+): , Eduardo Pondal 46, 986857784
7. H **Room** (€45+): , Filgueira Valverde 10, 986869550
8. H **Virgen del Camino** (€38+/48): , Virgen del Camino 53-55, 986855900
9. H **Galicia** (€60+/80+): , Avenida de Vigo 3, 986864411
10. H **Madrid** (€32+/45+): , Andrés Mellado 5, 986865180
11. H **Comercio** (€30+/40+): , Augusto González Besada 5, 986851217

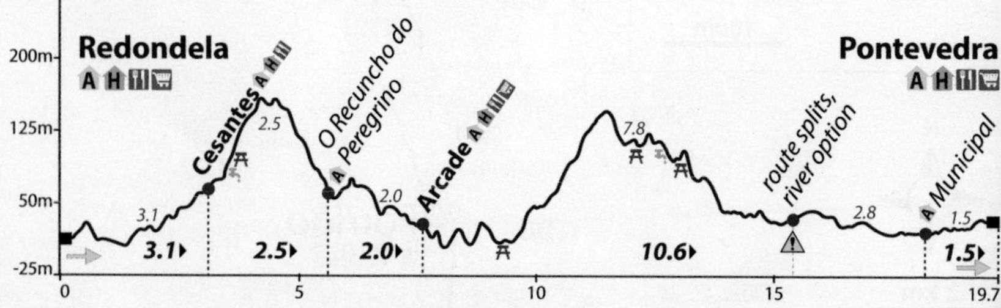

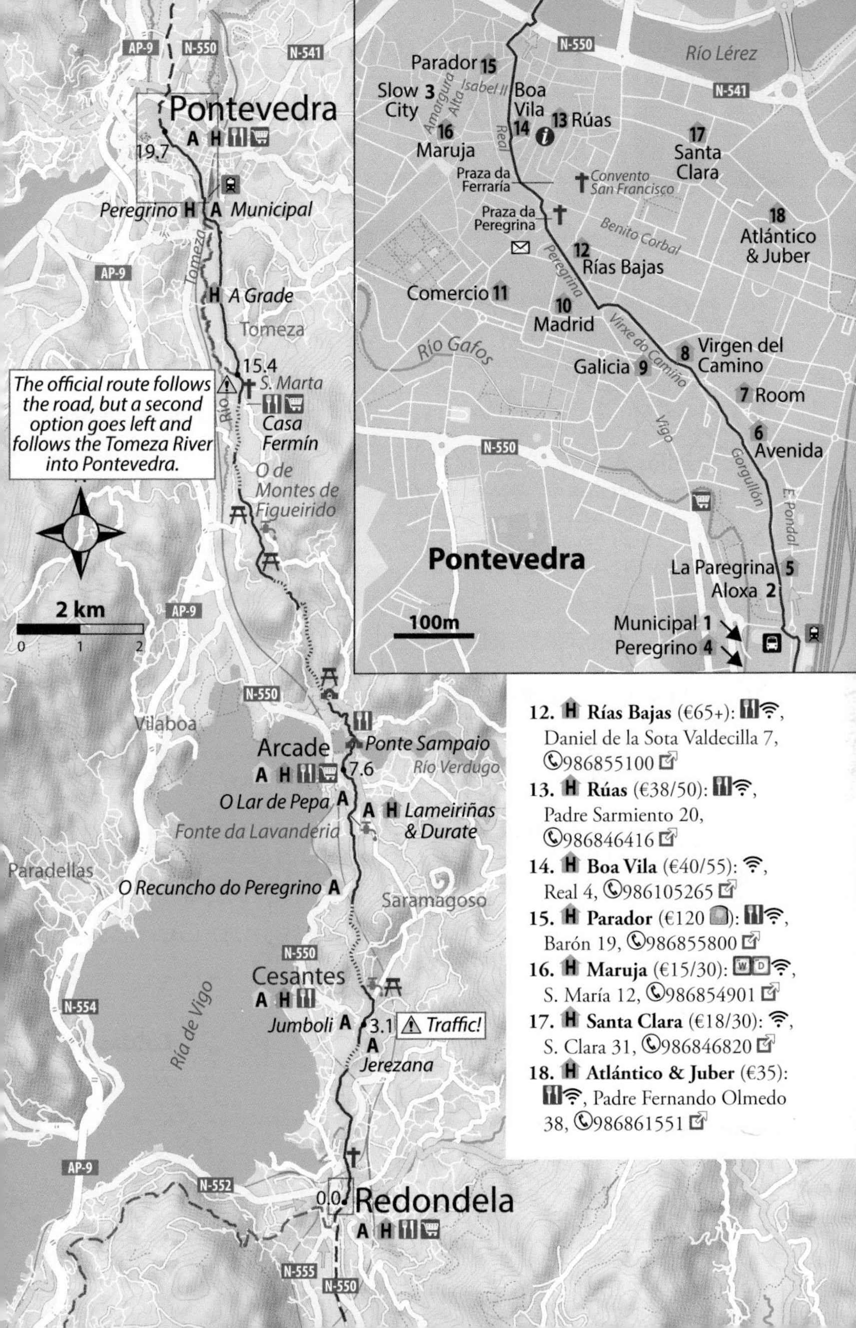

12. H **Rías Bajas** (€65+): Daniel de la Sota Valdecilla 7, 986855100

13. H **Rúas** (€38/50): Padre Sarmiento 20, 986846416

14. H **Boa Vila** (€40/55): Real 4, 986105265

15. H **Parador** (€120): Barón 19, 986855800

16. H **Maruja** (€15/30): S. María 12, 986854901

17. H **Santa Clara** (€18/30): S. Clara 31, 986846820

18. H **Atlántico & Juber** (€35): Padre Fernando Olmedo 38, 986861551

24 PONTEVEDRA TO CALDAS DE REIS

21.3km (13.2mi), 5.5-7 Hours, Difficulty:

P 67%, 14.2km, U 33%, 7.1km

Enjoy another day walking through the countryside, much of the time on cobblestone and dirt pathways. The detour to Barosa Falls (+1.3km) is worthwhile.

10.2 Portela/Barro A

Albergue is off-route on a road parallel to the Camino. After San Amaro, follow signs for A A Portela to R, while main route continues straight. Detour also leads to the beautiful Igrexa de Portela (easy connection to main route north of the church.)

A **A Portela** (16, €7): , 655952805, all year, café is +1.2km in San Amaro

16.6 Briallos A

No services other than the albergue. To reach the albergue (+350m), leave the route to the L and cross the river, before continuing on the paved road.

A **Briallos - Portas** (muni, 27, €6): , Lugar San Roque, 986536194, 1pm-10pm all year, no close services, but some restaurants deliver, +350m

19.5 Tivó A

A **Catro Canos** (18, €10): , Tivó 58, 696582014, 600345181

21.3 Caldas de Reis A H

1. A H **Timonel** (20, €8/-/20): , Herrería 3, 986540840, 696805305
2. A H **O Cruceiro** (40, €12/-/30): , Juan Fuentes 40, 986540165
3. A **Pousada Doña Urraca** (muni, 50, €6): , Campo da Torre 1, 669822529, 1pm-10pm all year, crowded and a bit run-down
4. H **O Cruceiro** (€30/45): , Juan Fuentes 40, 986540165, same owners/location as Albergue O Cruceiro
5. H **Balneario Acuña** (€50+/70+): , Herrería 2, 902104841
6. H **Balneario Dávila** (€32-35/52-55): , Laureano Salgado 11, 986540012
7. H **La Moderna** (€30): , Pedro Mateo Sagasta 9, 986540312, Apr 1-Nov 1
8. H **Lotus** (€40): , Dolores Mosquera 16, 986530650

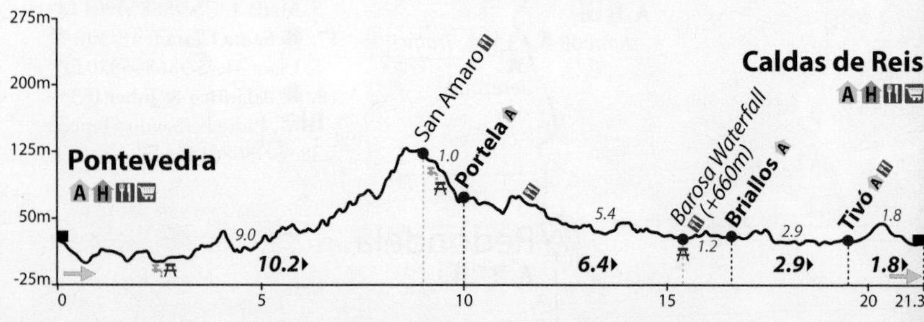

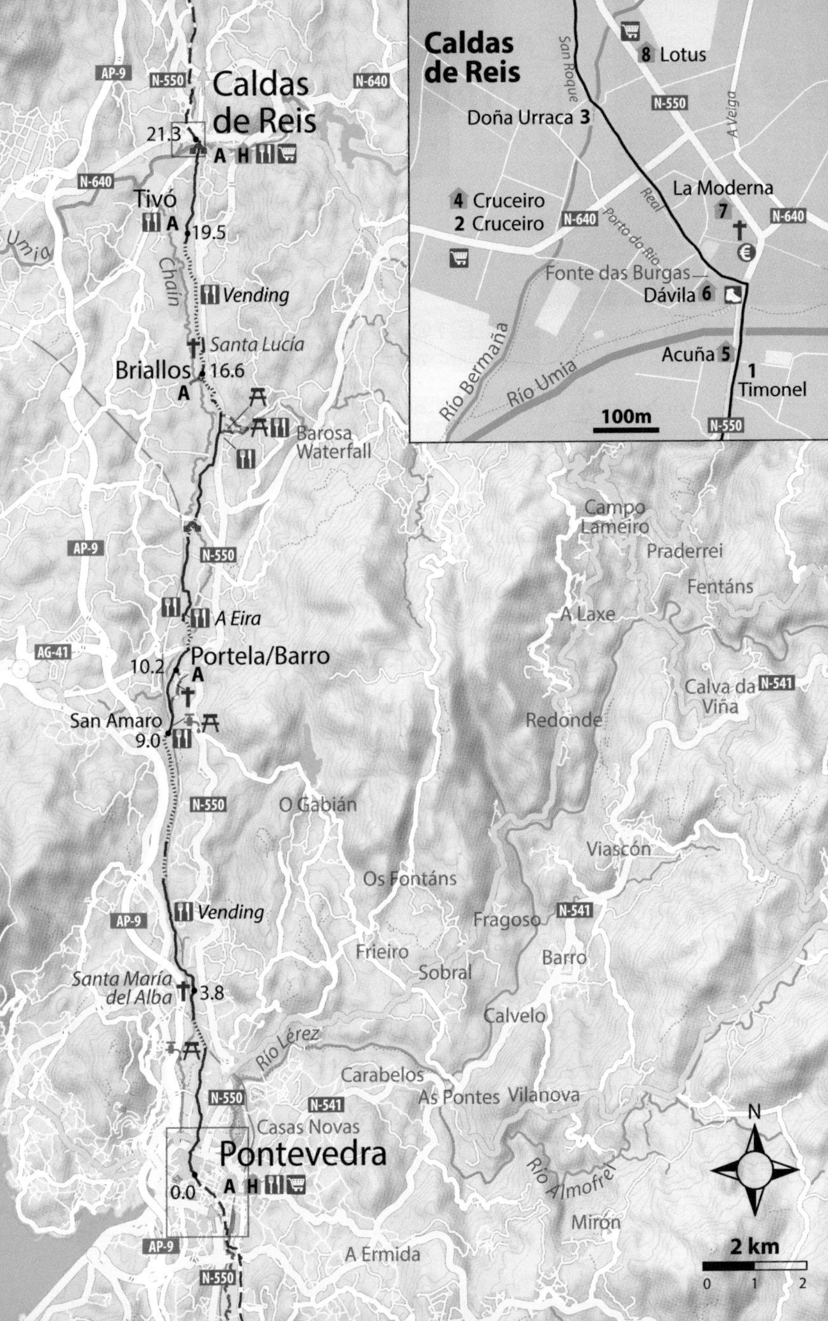
Caldas de Reis
Pontevedra
Tivó
Briallos
Portela/Barro
San Amaro
Santa María del Alba
Santa Lucía
Vending
A Eira
Barosa Waterfall
21.3
19.5
16.6
10.2
9.0
3.8
0.0
Chain
Umia
Río Lérez
Río Almofrei
Campo Lameiro
Praderrei
Fentáns
A Laxe
Calva da Viña
Redonde
O Gabián
Viascón
Os Fontáns
Fragoso
Frieiro
Sobral
Barro
Calvelo
Carabelos
As Pontes
Vilanova
Casas Novas
Mirón
A Ermida
AP-9
N-550
N-640
N-541
AG-41
2 km
0
1
2
N
Caldas de Reis
8 Lotus
Doña Urraca 3
4 Cruceiro
2 Cruceiro
La Moderna
7
Fonte das Burgas
Dávila 6
Acuña 5
1 Timonel
San Roque
Real
Porto do Río
A Veiga
Río Bermaña
Río Umia
100m

25 CALDAS DE REIS TO PADRÓN

18.9km (11.7mi), 5-6.5 Hours, Difficulty:

P 58%, 11.0km, U 42%, 7.9km

5.5 Carracedo H

H **Sevi** (€20): , Carracedo Cruceiro 32, 986534260, reception in António

9.8 Valga A

A **Valga** (muni, 78, €6): , Lugar de O Pino, 638943271, 1-10pm, all year, nicely maintained with ample space and pleasant, shaded yard in front

16.2 Pontecesures A H

A **Pontecesures** (muni, 54, €6): , Estrada Escolas, 699832730, 1-10pm
H **A Casa do Río** (€50): , Dr. Víctor García 1, 986557575

16.5 Herbón, +2.8 A

Herbón Detour: At T on northern edge of Pontecesures, follow red blazes R as yellow marks go L. Yellow marks lead back to Padrón path.

A **San Antonio de Herbón** (assoc, 30, don): , Convento de San Antonio, 881098102, 4-10pm Apr-Oct; peaceful; evening/morning mass; communal meals

18.9 Padrón A H

Name from Galician for "big stone," referring to the traditional mooring stone of the boat carrying St. James' body. † Santiaguiño do Monte chapel, 1.5km west of town, marks the traditional place of St. James' first sermon in Iberia.

1. A **Camiño do Sar** (20, €13-15): , Lugar Devesa 20, 618734373
2. A H **Flavia** (22, €12/25/38): , La Feria 13, 981810455, all y.
3. A H **A Barca de Pedra** (23, €13-14): , Vidal Cepeda 6, 981811112, Mar-Oct, room for only 3 bicycles
4. A **Padrón** (muni, 46, €6): , Costanilla del Carmen, 673656173, 1-10pm all year, nice location with views in beautiful historic building
5. A **Rossol** (18, €14): , Plaza Rodríguez Cobián 1, 981810011
6. A **Corredoiras** (26, €13-16): , Corredoira Barca 10, 981817266
7. H **Chef Rivera** (€29+/46+): , Enlace Parque 7, 981810413
8. H **Jardín** (€35-45): , Franco Salgado Araujo 3, 981810950
9. H **Pensión O Grilo** (€25/51): , Camilo José Cela 30, 981810607

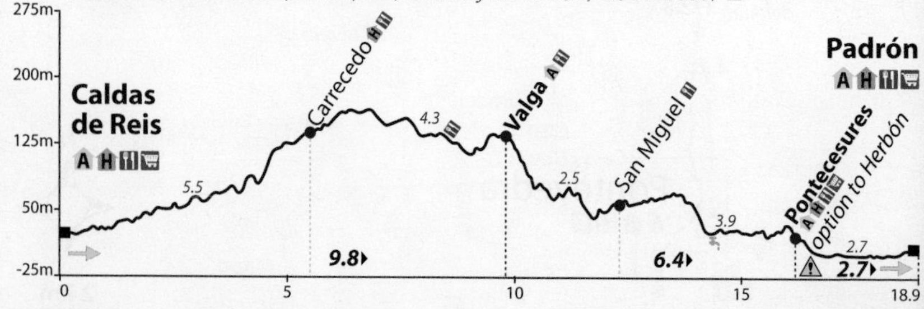

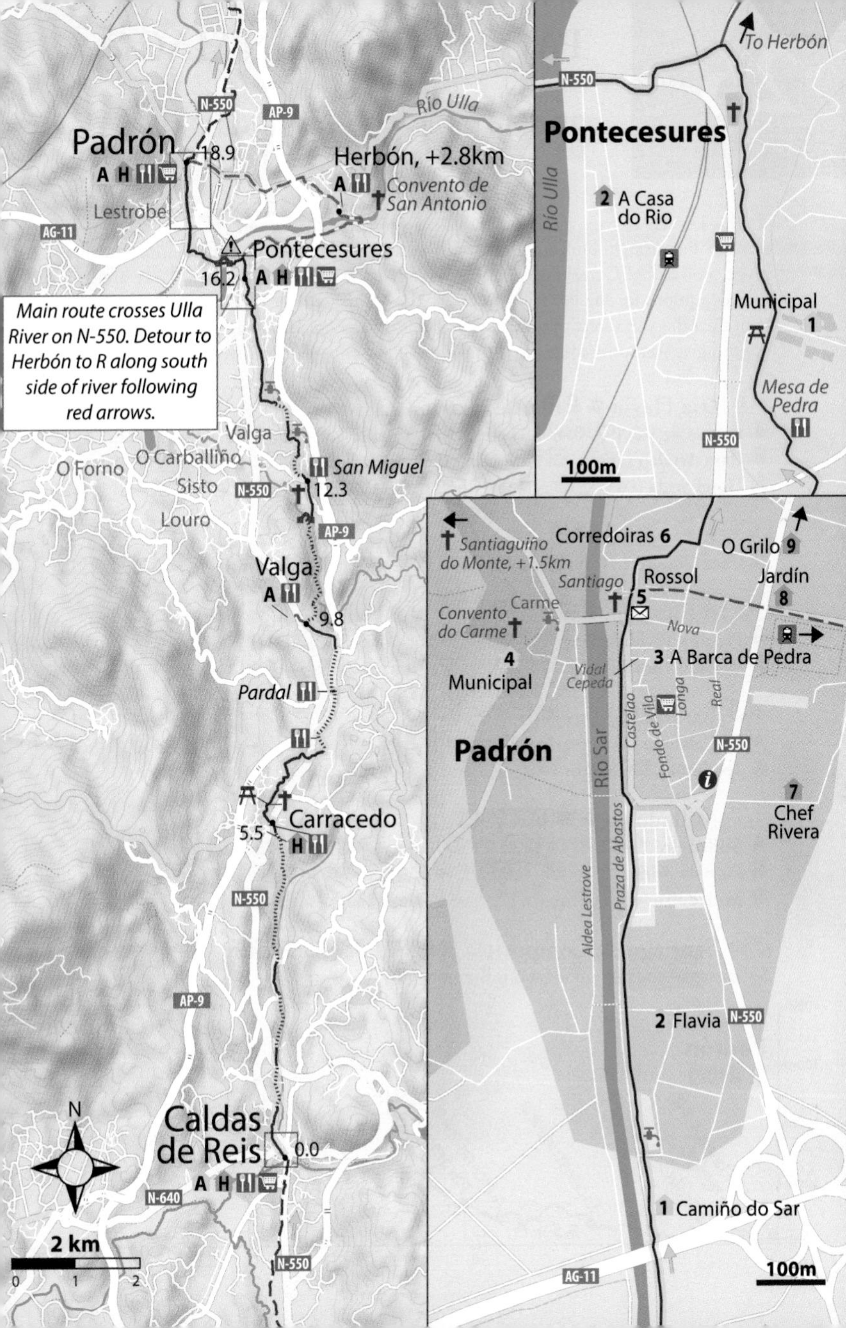

Padrón
18.9
N-550
AP-9
Río Ulla
Herbón, +2.8km
A
Convento de San Antonio
Lestrobe
AG-11
Pontecesures
16.2
A H
Main route crosses Ulla River on N-550. Detour to Herbón to R along south side of river following red arrows.
Valga
O Carballiño
O Forno
Sisto
Louro
San Miguel
12.3
Valga
A
9.8
Pardal
Carracedo
5.5
H
Caldas de Reis
0.0
N-640
N
2 km
0
1
2
To Herbón
Pontecesures
2 A Casa do Rio
Municipal
1
Mesa de Pedra
100m
Corredoiras 6
Santiaguiño do Monte, +1.5km
O Grilo 9
Jardín
8
Santiago
Rossol
5
Carme
Convento do Carme
Nova
3 A Barca de Pedra
4
Municipal
Vidal Cepeda
Castelao
Fondo de Vila
Longa
Real
Padrón
Río Sar
7
Chef Rivera
Aldea Lestrove
Praza de Abastos
2 Flavia
1 Camiño do Sar
100m

26 PADRÓN TO SANTIAGO

25.6km (15.9mi), 7-9 Hours, Difficulty:
P 83%, 21.2km, U 17%, 4.4km

This last day to Santiago is less scenic than some on the Camino Portugués, as you pass through increasingly built-up areas, but the thought of reaching your destination should prove motivating! Occasional stretches on dirt paths break up the day. There are several marked options for the last few kilometers into Santiago; none of which is decidedly better than the others. A direct option takes you to Santiago quickest, while other, slightly longer, options give you some additional dirt road walking along the Sar River.

1.0 Iria Flavia A H Just 1km beyond Padrón.
A **Cruces de Iria** (16, €12): Camilo José Cela 48, 649602092
H **Casa Arteleira** (€40): Lugar de Pedreda 1, 636931524
H **Hotel Scala** (€45/55): N-550 s/n, 981811312

6.3 Escravitude H
H **Casa Grande da Capellania** (€51/61): Lugar de A Esclavitude, 651132591

9.3 A Picaraña H
H **Pensión Pividal** (€25+/35+): Picaraña 10, 981803119
H **Pensión Glorioso** (€12-25/20-35): Picaraña 23, 981803181

10.5 Faramello/Teo A
A **La Calabaza del Peregrino** (36, €12): Faramello 5, 981194244, Apr-O
A **Teo** (muni, 28, €6): de Francos, 981815700

17.7 Milladoiro A H
A **Milladoiro** (62, €14): Buxo, 981938382
H **Pazo da Adrán** (€50+): Lugar de Adrán 4, 981570000
H **Milladoiro** (€35+): Anxeriz 12, 981536623, call ahead

25.6 Santiago de Compostela A H
See city map and accommodations list on p. 76-77.

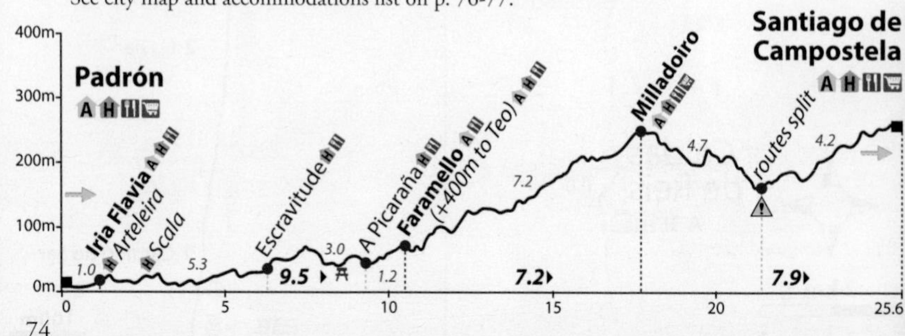

⚠ Alternative routes to enter Santiago
❶ Direct: Most direct, but misses walking on a dirt road along the Sar River.
2a Santa Marta: After following the Sar River on a dirt road 2a splits from 2b, crossing a bridge over SC-20 and continuing to Santiago via Santa Marta.
2b Conxo: Splits from 2a, going R before bridge over SC-20 and continuing to Santiago via Conxo.
N-550
Santiago de Campostela
25.6
Santa Marta
21.4
2a
2b
A Paradiña
N-550
Conxo
23.2
AG-56
Bertamiráns
Framil
AP-9
Milladoiro
17.7
Bugallido
San Salvador
Firmistáns
N-550
AC-841
Pedrouso
AP-53
A Ribeira
Texexe
Casa Rural Parada de Francos
Teo
Mouromorto
AP-9
a Calabaza del Peregrino
10.9
Teo
10.5
Faramello
AG-59
A Picaraña
9.3
O Areal
A Ramollosa
Bouñou
Escravitude
6.3
A Agrela
Loureiro
A Florida
Mosteiro
N-550
Río de Santa Lucía
Gaia
Sar
AP-9
Pontevea
Scala
Cruces de Iria
Casal
Casa Arteleira
Iria Flavia
1.0
Río Ulla
Padrón
0.0
Río Vea
N
AP-9
2 km
0
1
2

Santiago de Compostela

Meiga Backpackers 13
Basquinos 45 12
Carme
Santa Clara
11 La Salle
Parque de Domingos Bonaval
San Francisco
Altaïr 23
O Fogar de Teodomiro
Arte
24 Costa Vella
9 10 Linares
Das Rodas
Domingo
Pilgrim Office
1 Blanco
Galeras
San Martín Pinario 25
A Casa do Peregrino 7
Plaza Cervantes
Casa Reais
Dos Reis Católicos 26
6 Azabache
8 Last Stamp
Hortas
Police
Praza do Obradoiro
Cathedral
San Paio
Pilgrimage
Poza de Bar
To Finisterre and Muxía
2 Roots and Boots
Fonseca 27
Tourist Info (Galicia)
Mundoalbergue
Pombal
3
Vilar
Virxe da Cerca
Seminario Menor 14
Tourist Info (Santiago)
28 Suso
Parque Alameda
Susana
Parque Belvís
Senra
Xoan Carlos I
N
Montero Ríos
Cycling the Camino
Hórreo
200m
Praza Roxa
República Salvador
Rosalía de Castro
Repúblical Arxentina
2a
1
2b
Compostela 4
Ferrol
Vilagracia
Romero Donallo
La Estación 5

25. San Martín Pinario (pilgrim €23/40): Plaza Inmaculada, 981560282

26. Hostal Dos Reis Católicos (€160+/180+): Praza do Obradoiro, 981582200, Parador

27. Pensión Fonseca (€40/65): Fonseca 1, 981584145

28. Hostal Suso (€40-60): Villar 65, 981586611

25.6 **Santiago de Compostela** A H

Santiago city: Rúa do Vilar 63, 981-555129, Daily 9am-9pm (summer)

Galicia: Rúa do Vilar 30, 902-332010, M-F 10am-8pm, Sa 11am-2pm, 5-7pm, Su 11am-2pm

Pilgrim office: Rúa Carretas 33, 981-568846, Daily M-Sa 9am-9pm (summer), left luggage,

1. A H **Blanco** (20, €20/-/45): Galeras 30, 881976850
2. A **Roots and Boots** (hstl., 48, €14-21): Campo Cruceiro do Galo 7, 699631594
3. A **Mundoalbergue** (34, €16-18): San Clemente 26, 981588625, all year
4. A **Compostela** (36, €16): S Pedro de Mezonzo 28, 881017840
5. A H **La Estación** (24, €15/30/40): Xoana Nogueira 14, 981594624, all year
6. A **Azabache** (20, €14-18): Azabachería 15, 981071254, all year
7. A H **A Casa Do Peregrino** (€15-20/70/70): Azabacheria 2, 981573931
8. A **Last Stamp** (54, €18-25): Preguntoiro 10, 981563525, mid Jan-mid Dec
9. A **Fogar de Teodomiro** (hstl, 20, €18): Algalia de Arriba 3, 981582920, 10am
10. A H **Linares** (14, €22/60/70): Algalia Abajo 34, 981580443
11. A H **La Salle** (20, €18/27/59): Tras Santa Clara, 682158011
12. A **Basquinos 45** (10, €12-15): Basquinos 45, 661894536, all year
13. A **Meiga Backpackers** (hostel, 30, €11-13): Basquiños 67, 981570846, all year
14. A H **Seminario Menor** (177, €14/17/-): Quiroga Palacios 2, 881031768
15. A **Porta Real** (24, €10-20): Concheiros 10, 633610114, all year
16. A **La Estrella de Santiago** (24, €10-16): Concheiros 36-38, 881973926, all year
17. A **La Credential** (36, €15): Fonte d. Concheiros 13, 981068083, Mar-Nov
18. A **Monterrey** (36, €15): Fontiñas 65, 655484299, all year
19. A **Acuario** (70, €13-15): Estocolmo 2, 981575438, Mar-Nov
20. A **Santo Santiago** (40, €10-12): Lázaro Valiño 3, 657402403, all year
21. A **Fin del Camino** (assoc, 110, €9): Moscova, 981587324, May-Oct
22. A **Xunta** (80, €10 first night, €7 for 2nd/3rd): c/San Lázaro, 981571488, all year
23. H **Altaïr Hotel** (€75/110): Loureiros 12, 981554712
24. H **Costa Vella** (€60/83): Porta da Pena 17, 981569530, restored Jesuit house

COASTAL 16A

PORTO TO VILA DO CONDE

33.2km (20.6mi), 9-11.5 Hours, Difficulty:

P 59%, 19.6km, U 41%, 13.7km

The Coastal Route follows the Atlantic, generally near the coastline, before turning inland, following the Vigo River back to the Central Route in Redondela. The official route (2a) sometimes cuts inland, while the Senda Litoral (2b) continues along the coastline (see p. 53).

11.7 Matosinhos

H **Pensão Central** (€30-37/42): W D, Brito Capelo 599, 229380664

23.0 Angeiras

A **Camping Orbitur** (€8-14/14-20/40): K W D, Angeiras, 229270571, pilgrim dorm prices in shared bungalows; some bungalows have kitchens; +550m

23.9 Labruge

A **São Tiago de Labruge** (mun, 18, don): K, Labruge 1720, 961180256, pleasant, simple, well-maintained albergue; key: Betty in house across street; +880m

26.2 Vila Chã

A **São Mamede** (muni, 14, don): , Travessa do Sol, 229285607, 2-9pm

H **Residencial Sandra** (€25/35): W, Facho 30, 229283634, 917487512

33.2 Vila do Conde

1. A **Sta. Clara** (muni, 25, €8): K W D, 5 de Outubro 221, 252104717, 3-10pm
2. A H **Bellamar** (12, €10-16/20/35): K W D, República 84, 252631748
3. A H **Erva Doce** (6, €15/-/48): , Cais das Lavandeiras 39, 919058715
4. A **Two Double One** (6, €20): K, Com. António Fernandes 211, 912230442
5. H **Pensão Patarata**: Cais das Lavandeiras 18, 252631894
6. H **Brazão** (€40+/56+): , Dr. João Canavarro 1, 252642016
7. H **Casa Venceslau** (€45-50): , Mós 13, 252646362
8. H **A Princesa do Ave** (€35/45): , António José Sousa Pereira 261, 252642065
9. H **Santana Hotel & Spa** (€75+): W D, Monte Santana 188, 252640460

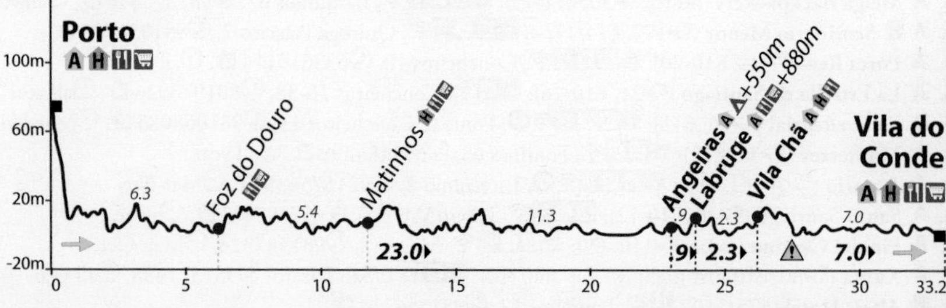

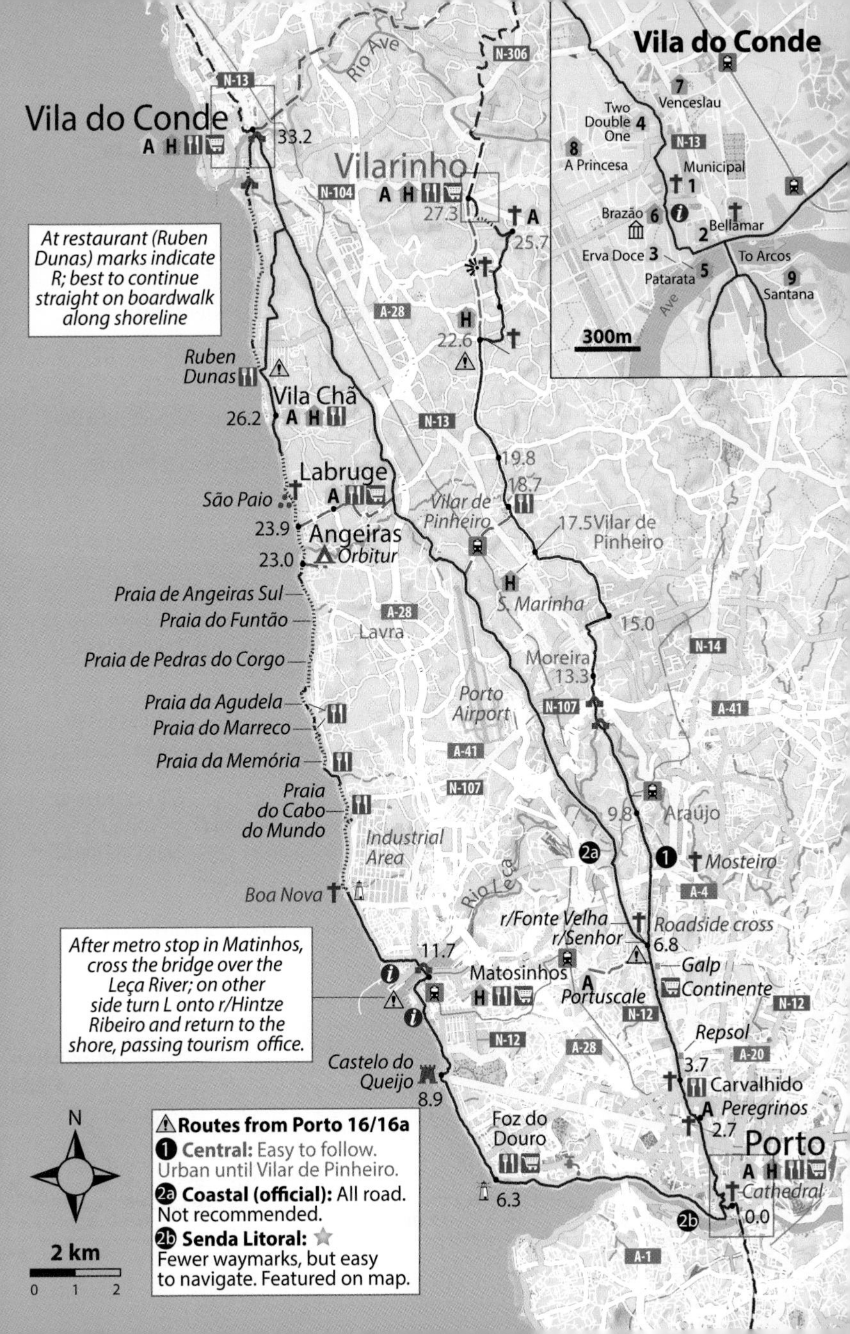

Vila do Conde
Vila do Conde
Two Double One 4
7 Venceslau
8 A Princesa
Municipal
1
Brazão 6
Bellamar 2
Erva Doce 3
Patarata 5
To Arcos
9 Santana
Ave
300m
N-13
N-306
Rio Ave
33.2
Vilarinho
N-104
27.3
25.7
22.6
At restaurant (Ruben Dunas) marks indicate R; best to continue straight on boardwalk along shoreline
Ruben Dunas
Vila Chã
26.2
A-28
N-13
19.8
18.7
Labruge
São Paio
23.9
Angeiras
Orbitur
23.0
Vilar de Pinheiro
17.5 Vilar de Pinheiro
S. Marinha
Praia de Angeiras Sul
Praia do Funtão
Lavra
15.0
N-14
Praia de Pedras do Corgo
Moreira
13.3
Porto Airport
Praia da Agudela
Praia do Marreco
N-107
A-41
Praia da Memória
N-107
Praia do Cabo do Mundo
9.8
Araújo
Industrial Area
2a
1
Mosteiro
A-4
Boa Nova
Rio Leça
r/Fonte Velha
Roadside cross
r/Senhor
6.8
Galp
After metro stop in Matinhos, cross the bridge over the Leça River; on other side turn L onto r/Hintze Ribeiro and return to the shore, passing tourism office.
11.7
Matosinhos
Portuscale
Continente
N-12
N-12
Repsol
N-12
A-28
A-20
3.7
Castelo do Queijo
8.9
Carvalhido
Peregrinos
2.7
Foz do Douro
Porto
Cathedral
6.3
0.0
2b
A-1
N
2 km
0 1 2
Routes from Porto 16/16a
1 Central: Easy to follow. Urban until Vilar de Pinheiro.
2a Coastal (official): All road. Not recommended.
2b Senda Litoral: Fewer waymarks, but easy to navigate. Featured on map.

COASTAL 17A

VILA DO CONDE TO MARINHAS

28.4km (17.6mi), 7-9.5 Hours, Difficulty:

P 81%, 22.9km, U 19%, 5.5km

4.0 **Póvoa de Varzim**

A **S. José de Ribamar** (par, 16, don): Mouzinho de Albuquerque 32, 252622314, 2pm-8pm, keys in São José de Ribamar Church (same street)

A H **Hostel Sardines and Friends** (€20/-/40+): Ponte 4, 962083329

H **Luso Brasileiro** (€40/50): Cafés 16, 252690710

H **Grande Hotel** (€54/60): Alegre 20, 252290400

9.3 H **Santo André** (€55-75): Santo André Aver-O-Mar, 252615666

14.9 H **Orbitur Rio Alto** (€14-20): Rio Alto, 252615699

17.8 **Apúlia** H

H **Apúlia Praia** (€43+/57+): Praia 45, 253989290, +740m

21.4 **Fão**

A H **Foz do Cávado** (91, €10/-/29): Alameda Bom Jesus, 253982045

H **Parque do Rio** (€40-80/50-90): Padre Manuel de Sá Pereira, 253981521

24.1 **Esposende**

1. A H **Hostel Eleven** (14, €10/-/42): Narciso Ferreira 57, 253039303
2. A H **Esposende Guest House** (8, €12/35/50): Conde Agrolongo 29, 932832818
3. A **GoKiteSurf Guesthouse** (6, €16): Nossa Sra. da Graça, 934179024
4. H **Mira Rio** (€40): Ponte D. Luis Filipe 113, 253964430
5. H **Suave Mar** (€55/54-61): Eng. Eduardo Arantes e Oliv., 253969400

28.4 **Marinhas**

A **São Miguel das Marinhas** (34, don): São Sebastião, 253964720

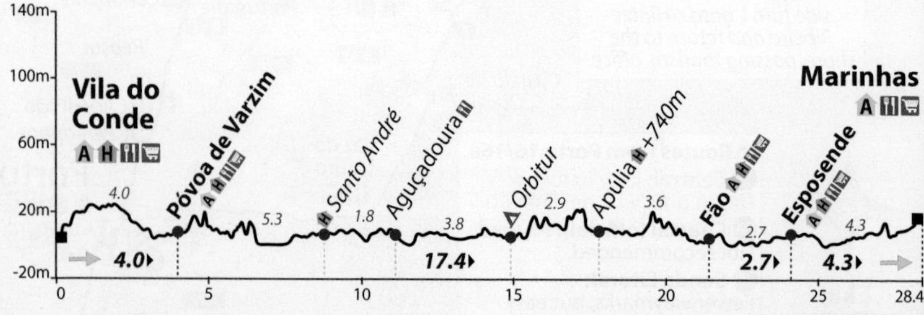

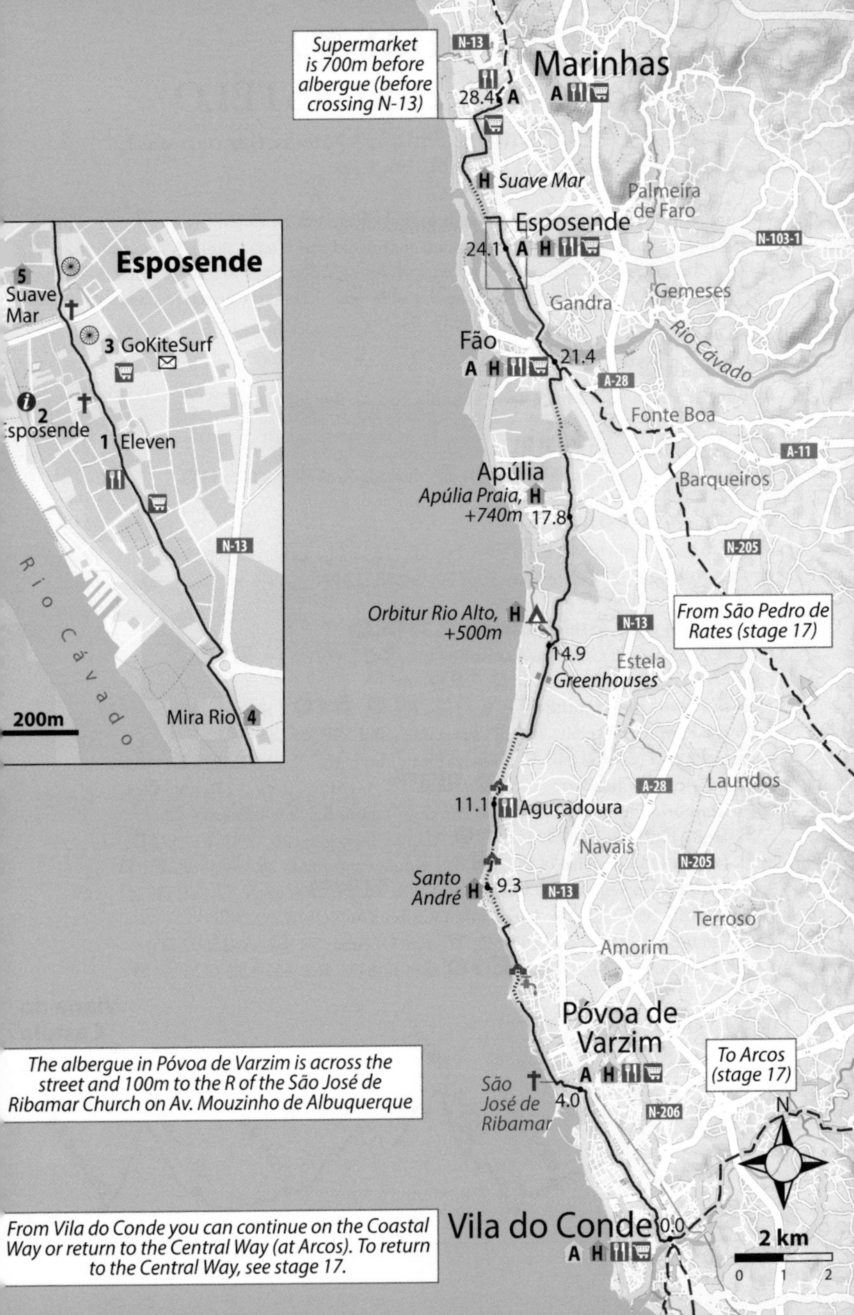

Supermarket is 700m before albergue (before crossing N-13)
N-13
Marinhas
28.4
Suave Mar
Palmeira de Faro
Esposende
N-103-1
24.1
Gandra
Gemeses
Rio Cávado
Fão
21.4
A-28
Fonte Boa
A-11
Apúlia
Apúlia Praia, +740m
17.8
Barqueiros
N-205
From São Pedro de Rates (stage 17)
Orbitur Rio Alto, +500m
N-13
14.9
Estela
Greenhouses
A-28
Laundos
11.1
Aguçadoura
Navais
N-205
Santo André
9.3
N-13
Terroso
Amorim
Póvoa de Varzim
To Arcos (stage 17)
São José de Ribamar
4.0
N-206
N
Vila do Conde
0.0
2 km
0
1
2
Esposende
5 Suave Mar
3 GoKiteSurf
2 Esposende
1 Eleven
N-13
Rio Cávado
200m
Mira Rio 4
The albergue in Póvoa de Varzim is across the street and 100m to the R of the São José de Ribamar Church on Av. Mouzinho de Albuquerque
From Vila do Conde you can continue on the Coastal Way or return to the Central Way (at Arcos). To return to the Central Way, see stage 17.

COASTAL
18A

MARINHAS TO VIANA DO CASTELO

20.5km (12.7mi), 5-7 Hours, Difficulty:
75%, 15.4km, 25%, 5.1km

From Marinhas, enjoy walking through coastal villages. Be careful crossing N-13 as the intersection has poor visibility (a new detour may avoid this intersection). A beautiful stone walking bridge leads across the Neiva River, with forested dirt roads to follow. Viana do Castelo is a beautiful town. Consider walking the additional 9.2km to Carreço to stay in a more rural location, such as Casa do Sardão (p. 84).

13.4 Chafé

Casa da Reina (€60): , Pardinheiro 122, 258351882

15.8 Vila Nova Anha

Quinta do Paço d' Anha (€55+/70+): Estrada Real, 258322459

18.3 Darque

Do Cais (€15/-/45+): , Estrada Nacional 13, 258331031
Don Augusto: , Travessa Anturios 60, 258322491

20.5 Viana do Castelo

1. **São João da Cruz dos Caminhos** (par, 20, €6/15/25): , Igreja do Carmo, 258822264, 2:30pm
2. **Posada de Juventude** (70, €10/-/26+): , Limia, 258838458
3. **Do Parque** (€40+/50+): , Praça da Galiza, 258828605
4. **Calatrava** (€45/60): , Manuel Fiúza Júnior 157, 258828911
5. **Fabrica do Chocolate** (€95+): , Gontim 70, 258244000
6. **Zimborio Guest House** (€35+): , Gago Coutinho, 938354863
7. **Dona Emília** (€54+): , Manuel Espregueira 6, 917811392
8. **Pensão O Laranjeiro** (€34+): , Manuel Espregueira 24, 258822258
9. **Hospedaria Senhora do Carmo** (€25-30): , Grande 72, 258825118
10. **Jardim** (€45+): , Largo 5 de Outubro 68, 258828915
11. **Margarida Da Praca** (€65-80): , 5 de Outubro 58, 965526692
12. **Laranjeira** (€44/50): , Cândido dos Reis 45, 258822261

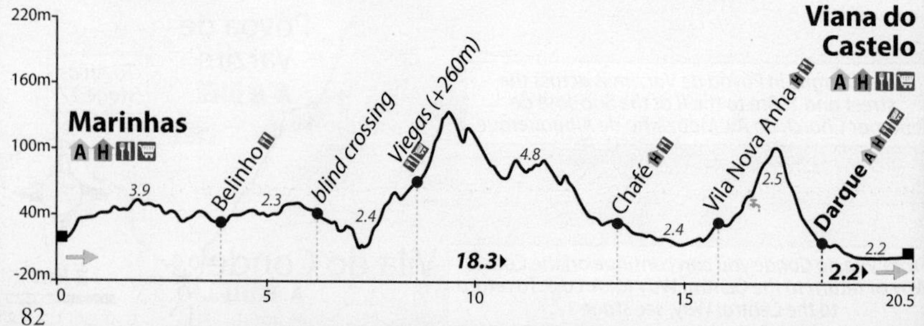

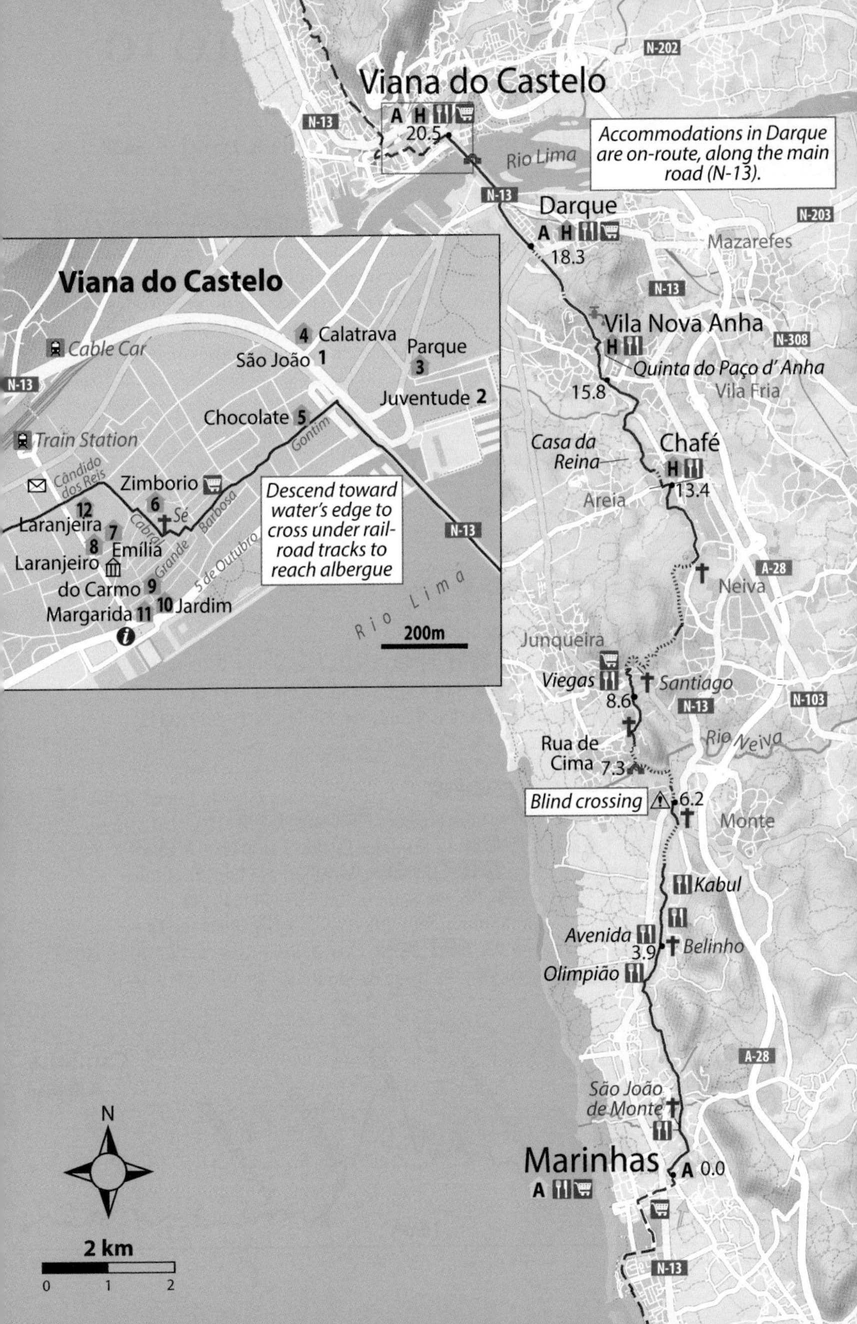

Viana do Castelo
A H
20.5
Rio Lima
Accommodations in Darque are on-route, along the main road (N-13).
N-202
N-13
N-203
Darque
A H
18.3
Mazarefes
Vila Nova Anha
H
Quinta do Paço d' Anha
N-308
15.8
Vila Fria
Chafé
Casa da Reina
H
13.4
Areia
A-28
Neiva
Junqueira
Viegas
Santiago
8.6
N-103
Rio Neiva
Rua de Cima
7.3
Blind crossing
6.2
Monte
Kabul
Avenida
3.9
Belinho
Olimpião
São João de Monte
Marinhas
A 0.0
A
N
2 km
0
1
2
Viana do Castelo
Cable Car
Train Station
4 Calatrava
São João 1
Parque
3
Juventude 2
Chocolate 5
Gontim
Cândido dos Reis
Zimborio
6
Sé
12
Laranjeira 7
8 Emília
Laranjeiro
do Carmo 9
Margarida 11
10 Jardim
Cabral
Grande
Barbosa
5 de Outubro
Descend toward water's edge to cross under railroad tracks to reach albergue
Rio Lima
200m

COASTAL **19A**

VIANA DO CASTELO TO CAMINHA

28.4km (17.6mi), 7.5-10 Hours, Difficulty:

P 83%, 23.6km, U 17%, 4.8km

It's possible to walk the shore from Viana do Castelo to Vila Praia de Âncora, but the official route leads along pleasant hillside, cobblestone roads and lovely villages. Along the coast, you also miss some views. Once in Caminha, stay in town or continue by ferry to A Guarda, Spain. Ferries runs from 9am weekdays and 10am on weekends (details in 20A). If you like an early start, consider staying in A Guarda instead of Caminha. In addition to the ferry, local boat owners will transport pilgrims across the Miño; check in the tourism office to connect. When you arrive in Spain, remember to turn your clocks forward an hour and use the Spanish country code +34 when making calls.

5.5 H **Quinta da Boa Viagem** (€60): , Quinta Boa Viagem, 935835835

9.2 Carreço A H

A H **Casa do Sardão** (20, €12/-/30): , Paço 769, 961790759, all year, shuttle to store

H **Casa do Nato** (€65-70/70-75): , Moreno 130, 258834041

19.2 Âncora A H

A H **D'Avenida** (18, €15/-/60): , Ramos Pereira 353, 258407764

H **Meira** (€65+/80+): , 5 de Outubro 56, 258911111

H **Albergaria Quim Barreiros** (€41+): Dr. Ramos Pereira 115, 258959100

H **Abrigo** (€40): , Pescadores 22, 258911577

28.4 Caminha A H

1. A **Municipal** (30, €5): , Padre Pinheiro, 914290431
2. H **Camarido** (€55+): , L. Joaninha, 258722130, SW of town
3. H **Camping Orbitur** (€40): , 258921295, SW of town
4. H **Arca Nova** (€25-30/35-40): , Dr. Sidónio Pais, 935390402
5. H **Residencial Galo D`ouro** (€30/40): , Corredoura 15, 258921160
6. H **Design & Wine** (€108/120): , Consel. Silva Torres 8, 258719040
7. H **Muralha de Caminha** (€70+): , Barão de São Roque 69, 258728199

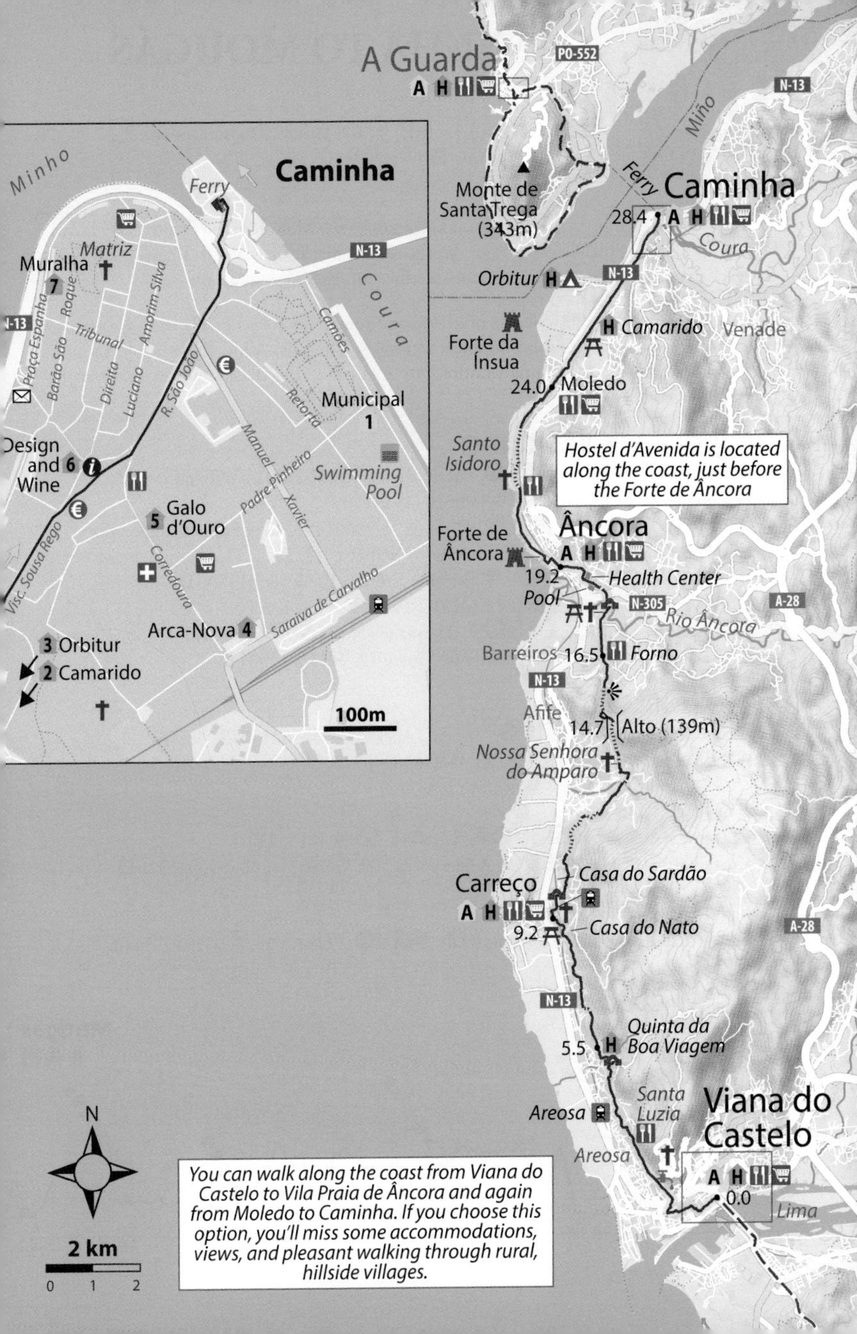
A Guarda
PO-552
N-13
Miño
Monte de Santa Trega (343m)
Ferry
Caminha
28.4
Coura
Orbitur
Camarido
Venade
Forte da Ínsua
24.0
Moledo
Santo Isidoro
Hostel d'Avenida is located along the coast, just before the Forte de Âncora
Forte de Âncora
Âncora
19.2
Health Center
Pool
N-305
Rio Âncora
A-28
Barreiros
16.5
Forno
Afife
14.7
Alto (139m)
Nossa Senhora do Amparo
Carreço
Casa do Sardão
9.2
Casa do Nato
Quinta da Boa Viagem
5.5
Santa Luzia
Areosa
Viana do Castelo
0.0
Lima
N
2 km
0 1 2
You can walk along the coast from Viana do Castelo to Vila Praia de Âncora and again from Moledo to Caminha. If you choose this option, you'll miss some accommodations, views, and pleasant walking through rural, hillside villages.
Caminha
Minho
Ferry
Matriz
Muralha 7
Praça Espanha
Barão São Roque
Tribunal
Direita
Luciano
Amorim Silva
R. São João
Camões
Coura
Retorta
Municipal 1
Swimming Pool
Design and Wine 6
Galo d'Ouro 5
Padre Pinheiro
Manuel Xavier
Corredoura
Visc. Sousa Rego
Saraiva de Carvalho
Arca-Nova 4
3 Orbitur
2 Camarido
100m

COASTAL
20A CAMINHA TO MOUGÁS

23.2km (14.4mi), 6-8 Hours, Difficulty:

P 70%, 16.3km, U 30%, 6.9km

A ferry from the northern edge of Caminha crosses the Miño River to Spain. Ferry leaves 9am-7pm approximately every hour. Weekends the first ferry leaves at 10am. Local boat owners can provide transport; check tourism office for schedule and details.

Once in Spain, you can walk the official inland route, uphill and briefly through a eucalyptus forest; or follow the shore (initially southwest along the Miño River before turning north and following the Atlantic coastline) to A Guarda. The coastal option, while more scenic, adds 3.0km.

3.8 A Guarda A H

1. A **Municipal** (36, €5): Puerto Rico 7, 986610025, 696986515
2. H **Celta** (€58): Galicia 53, 986610445
3. H **Bruselas** (€25-30/42-48): Ourense, 986614521, pilgrim's single price
4. H **Vila da Guarda** (€55): Tomiño 8, 986611121
5. H **Eli-Mar** (€33-53/45-64): Vicente Sobrino 12, 986613000
6. H **Convento de San Benito** (€48-61/51-78): Plaza San Benito, 986611166
7. H **Hostal del Mar** (€35): W D, Hermanos Noya, 986610638
8. H **Brisamar** (€40): Donantes de Sangre 72, 986613901

16.7 Oia H

H **Casa Puertas** (€45+): W D, Vicente López 7, 986362144, dbl €60

H **A Raíña** (€42+/53+): A Riña 21, 986362908

20.4 Viladesuso H

H **Glasgow** (€60+): W D, Serrallo 9, 986361552

H **Costa Verde** (€50+): A Serra Seca 103, 986361856, 696045326

23.2 Mougás A H

A H **Aguncheiro** (18, €10/-/20-40): O Porto 53, 665840774

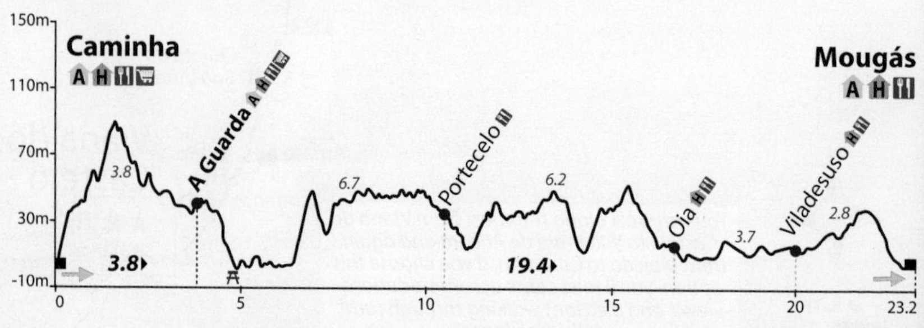

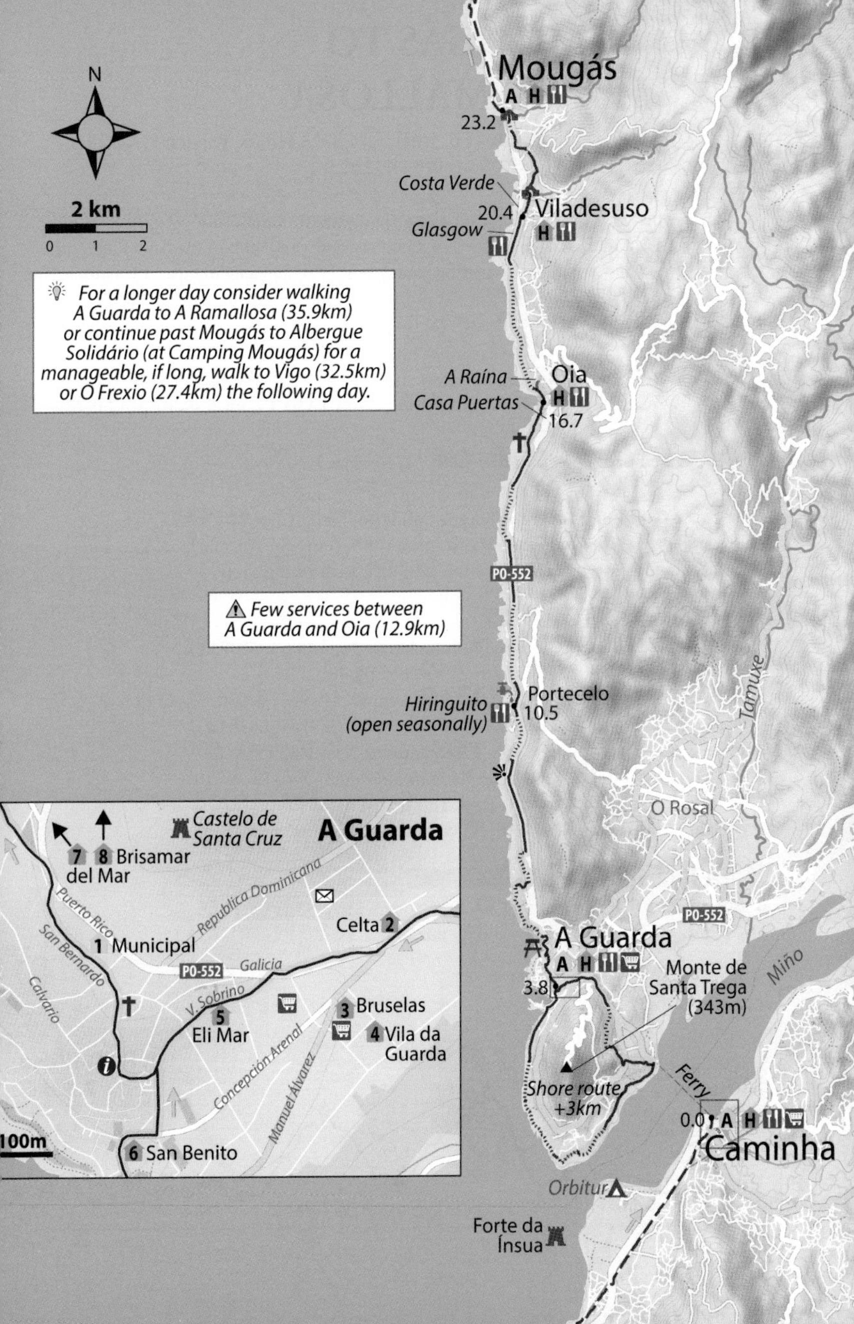

N
2 km
0 1 2
For a longer day consider walking A Guarda to A Ramallosa (35.9km) or continue past Mougás to Albergue Solidário (at Camping Mougás) for a manageable, if long, walk to Vigo (32.5km) or O Frexio (27.4km) the following day.
Few services between A Guarda and Oia (12.9km)
Mougás
23.2
Costa Verde
Viladesuso
20.4
Glasgow
A Raína
Oia
Casa Puertas
16.7
PO-552
Portecelo
Hiringuito (open seasonally)
10.5
Tamuxe
O Rosal
A Guarda
3.8
Monte de Santa Trega (343m)
Miño
Ferry
Shore route +3km
0.0
Caminha
Orbitur
Forte da Ínsua
A Guarda
Castelo de Santa Cruz
7 8 Brisamar
del Mar
Puerto Rico
Republica Dominicana
San Bernardo
Calvario
1 Municipal
Celta 2
Galicia
V. Sobrino
5 Eli Mar
3 Bruselas
4 Vila da Guarda
Concepción Arenal
Manuel Álvarez
100m
6 San Benito

COASTAL

21A

MOUGÁS TO A RAMALLOSA

16.5km (10.3mi), 4.5-6.5 HOURS, DIFFICULTY:

P 83%, 13.7km, U 17%, 2.8km

Today begins with a beautiful stroll along the coast. Be careful not to miss your turn (just before As Mariñas, 5.2km into the stage) for a wonderful climb to the day's high point (a manageable 113m ascent) with beautiful views of the coast and a lighthouse. The latter half of the day is more built up, but on the way down to O Sinal be sure to stop and take in views of the Cíes Islands at the mouth of the Vigo River.

1.5 **Camping O Muiño** (bungalow 1-4 persons: €35): , Carretera Baiona - A Guarda, Km 26, 986361600, Apr 1-Oct 15, small shop open July/Aug

1.8 **O Peñasco** (€40+): , Las Mariñas 115, 986361565

4.6 **Camping Mougás/Albergue Solidario** (40, €7+): , Carretera As Mariñas, 660596072, price is €7 plus nonperishable food donation (for local food pantry); you can buy the food item in the camp shop

11.6 **Baiona**

1. **Carabela La Pinta** (€45/65): , Entrehortas 21, 986355107
2. **Pinzón** (€30/40): , Elduayen 21, 986356046
3. **Tres Carabelas** (€25/40): , Ventura Misa 61, 986355441
4. **Anunciada** (€43/60): , Ventura Misa 58, 986356018
5. **Pensión Mosquito** (€25/40): , Elduayen 3, 986355036
6. **Cais** (€40+/60+): , Alférez Barreiro 3, 986355643
7. **Rompeolas** (€60/80): , Joselín 8, 615140220
8. **Santa Marta Playa** (€25/40): , Santa Marta 6, 986356045

16.5 **A Ramallosa**

Pazo Pias (50, €15): , Da Cabreira 21, 986350654, twin beds for pilgrims in single and double rooms

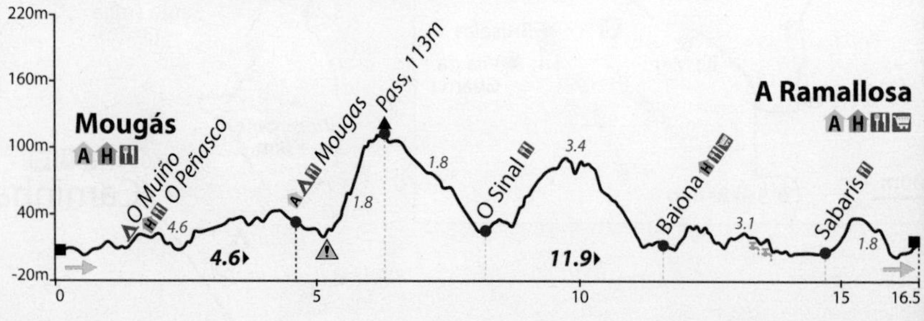

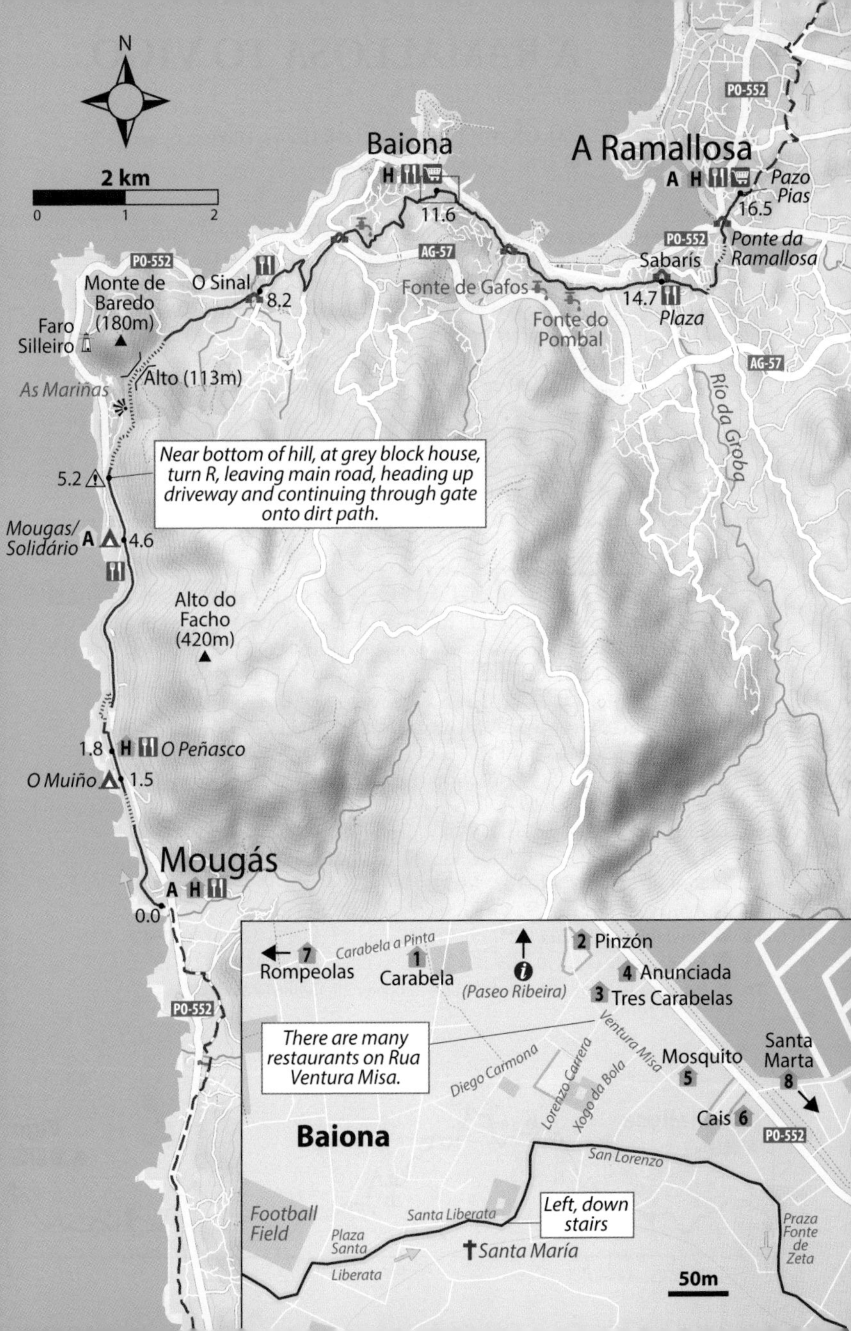
N
2 km
0
1
2
Baiona
A Ramallosa
PO-552
Pazo
Pias
11.6
16.5
Ponte da
Ramallosa
AG-57
Sabarís
Monte de
Baredo
(180m)
O Sinal
8.2
Fonte de Gafos
14.7
Plaza
Fonte do
Pombal
Faro
Silleiro
Alto (113m)
As Mariñas
Río da Groba
Near bottom of hill, at grey block house, turn R, leaving main road, heading up driveway and continuing through gate onto dirt path.
5.2
Mougas/
Solidário
4.6
Alto do
Facho
(420m)
1.8
O Peñasco
O Muiño
1.5
Mougás
0.0
Carabela a Pinta
7 Rompeolas
1 Carabela
(Paseo Ribeira)
2 Pinzón
4 Anunciada
3 Tres Carabelas
Ventura Misa
There are many restaurants on Rua Ventura Misa.
Diego Carmona
Lorenzo Carrera
Xogo da Bola
Mosquito 5
Santa Marta 8
Cais 6
Baiona
San Lorenzo
Football Field
Santa Liberata
Left, down stairs
Plaza Santa
Liberata
Santa María
Praza Fonte de Zeta
50m

COASTAL

22A

A RAMALLOSA TO VIGO

20.6km (12.8mi), 6-8 Hours, Difficulty:

71%, 14.6km, 29%, 6.0km

Today's route takes you back into built-up urban sprawl. Occasional sections of dirt road provide a respite from the pavement, and a pleasant dirt path along the Lagares River takes you into Vigo. There are many different route options and trail markings along the way today; the map highlights the two main options. The official route runs 20.6km into Vigo, but 10.2km into the day you can turn right, angling into the hills to O Freixo albergue. An alternative route follows the coast all the way to Vigo. Along this route, where the Lagares River meets the Vigo River, you can follow the Lagares inland to rejoin the official route.

3.3 H **Pensión Nigrán** (€30): , Telleira 33, 649747830

15.5 O Freixo A - Alternate Route

A **Refugio Peregrino O Freixo** (assoc, 8, don): , 679652431, limited space, reserve

20.6 Vigo A H

1. A H **Kaps** (20, €16+/-/53): , Emilia Pardo Bazán 12, 986110010
2. H **Tryp Los Galeones** (€60/80): , Madrid 21, 912764747, gym
3. H **Hostal Pío V** (€25): Vázquez Varela 46, 986410060
4. H **Oca Ipanema** (€35/40): , Vázquez Varela 31-33, 986471344
5. H **Celta** (€30/35): , México 22, 986414699
6. H **Casablanca** (€30/40): , México 7, 986482712
7. H **Zenit Vigo** (€50/60): , Gran Vía 1, 986417255
8. H **México** (€35/45): Vía Nte 10, 986431666
9. H **Solpor** (€36): , Vía Norte 9, 986416036 2
10. H **Junquera** (€52/68): , Uruguay 19, 986434888
11. H **Lar Atlántica** (€35/50): , Urzaiz 83, 986228245
12. H **Real** (€25/30): , Real 22, 699621449
13. H **Águila** (€27/42): , Victoria 6, 98643139
14. H **Hostal La Colegiata** (€25/35): , Plaza de la Iglesia 3, 986220129
15. H **Compostela** (€40/50): , García Olloqui 5, 986228227
16. H **Nautico** (€27/38): , Luis Taboada 28, 986122440

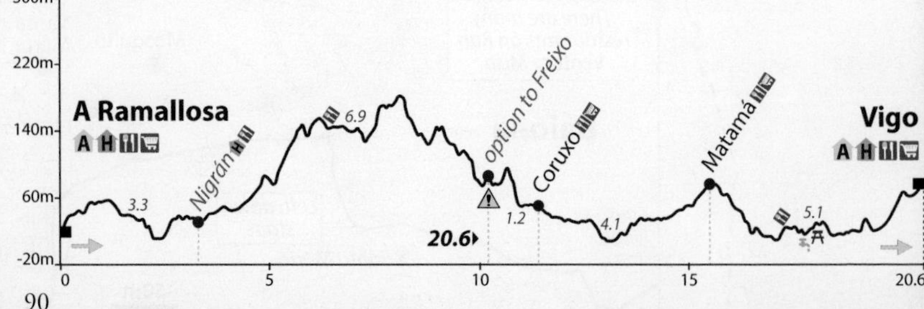

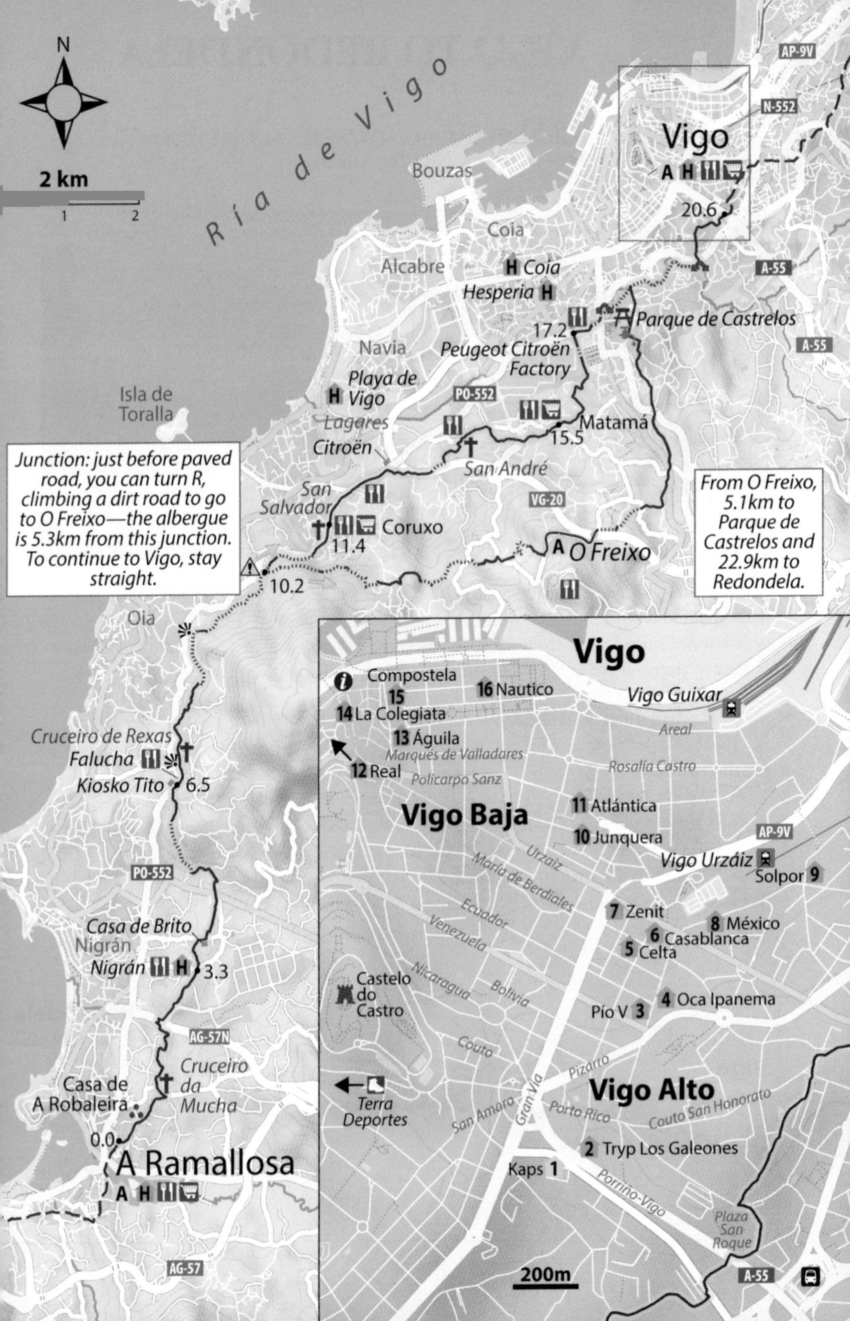

N
2 km
1
2
Ría de Vigo
Vigo
A H
20.6
AP-9V
N-552
A-55
Bouzas
Coia
Alcabre
H Coia
Hesperia H
17.2
Parque de Castrelos
Navia
Peugeot Citroën Factory
Playa de Vigo
H
Isla de Toralla
PO-552
Lagares
Citroën
Matamá
15.5
San André
San Salvador
Coruxo
11.4
VG-20
A O Freixo
From O Freixo, 5.1km to Parque de Castrelos and 22.9km to Redondela.
Junction: just before paved road, you can turn R, climbing a dirt road to go to O Freixo—the albergue is 5.3km from this junction. To continue to Vigo, stay straight.
10.2
Oia
Cruceiro de Rexas
Falucha
Kiosko Tito
6.5
PO-552
Casa de Brito
Nigrán
Nigrán
H
3.3
AG-57N
Cruceiro da Mucha
Casa de A Robaleira
0.0
A Ramallosa
A H
AG-57
Vigo
Compostela
15
16 Nautico
14 La Colegiata
13 Águila
Marqués de Valladares
12 Real
Policarpo Sanz
Vigo Guixar
Areal
Rosalía Castro
Vigo Baja
11 Atlántica
10 Junquera
AP-9V
Urzaiz
María de Berdiales
Vigo Urzáiz
Solpor 9
Ecuador
Venezuela
7 Zenit
6 Casablanca
8 México
5 Celta
Castelo do Castro
Nicaragua
Bolivia
4 Oca Ipanema
Pío V 3
Couto
Terra Deportes
Pizarro
Vigo Alto
Gran Vía
San Amaro
Porto Rico
Couto San Honorato
2 Tryp Los Galeones
Kaps 1
Porriño-Vigo
Plaza San Roque
200m
A-55

COASTAL
23A VIGO TO REDONDELA

15.5km (9.6mi), 4.5-6 Hours, Difficulty:
P 68%, 10.5km, U 32%, 5.0km

This is the last day on the Coastal Route. The route rejoins the Central Route in Redondela. You'll find few services between Vigo and Redondela, so plan accordingly. While you've now traveled inland, away from the coast, there are still spectacular views of the Vigo River—be sure to stop and enjoy them! For the next stage from Redondela see Stage 23 on p. 68.

15.5 Redondela

The Coastal Route returns to the Central Route in Redondela,where the number of pilgrims increases dramatically for the rest of the way to Santiago.

1. A **Casa da Torre** (34, €6): Praza de Ribadavia, 986404196
2. A H **Casa da Herba** (24, €10-12/-/40): Pr. Alfóndiga, 644404074
3. A **Rosa d'Abreu** (6, €15): Isidoro Queimaliños 33, 688422701
4. A **El Camino** (40, €10-12): Telmo Bernadez 11, 650963676
5. H **Alvear** (€40+/50+): Pai Crespo 30, 986400637
6. H **Rua do Medio** (€20/38): Reveriano Soutullo 46, 666764908

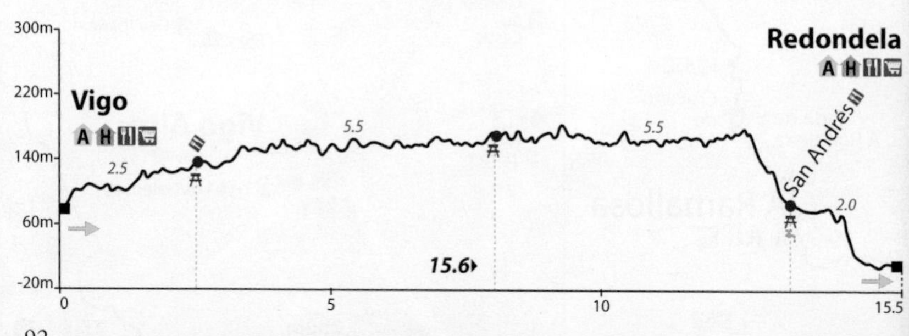

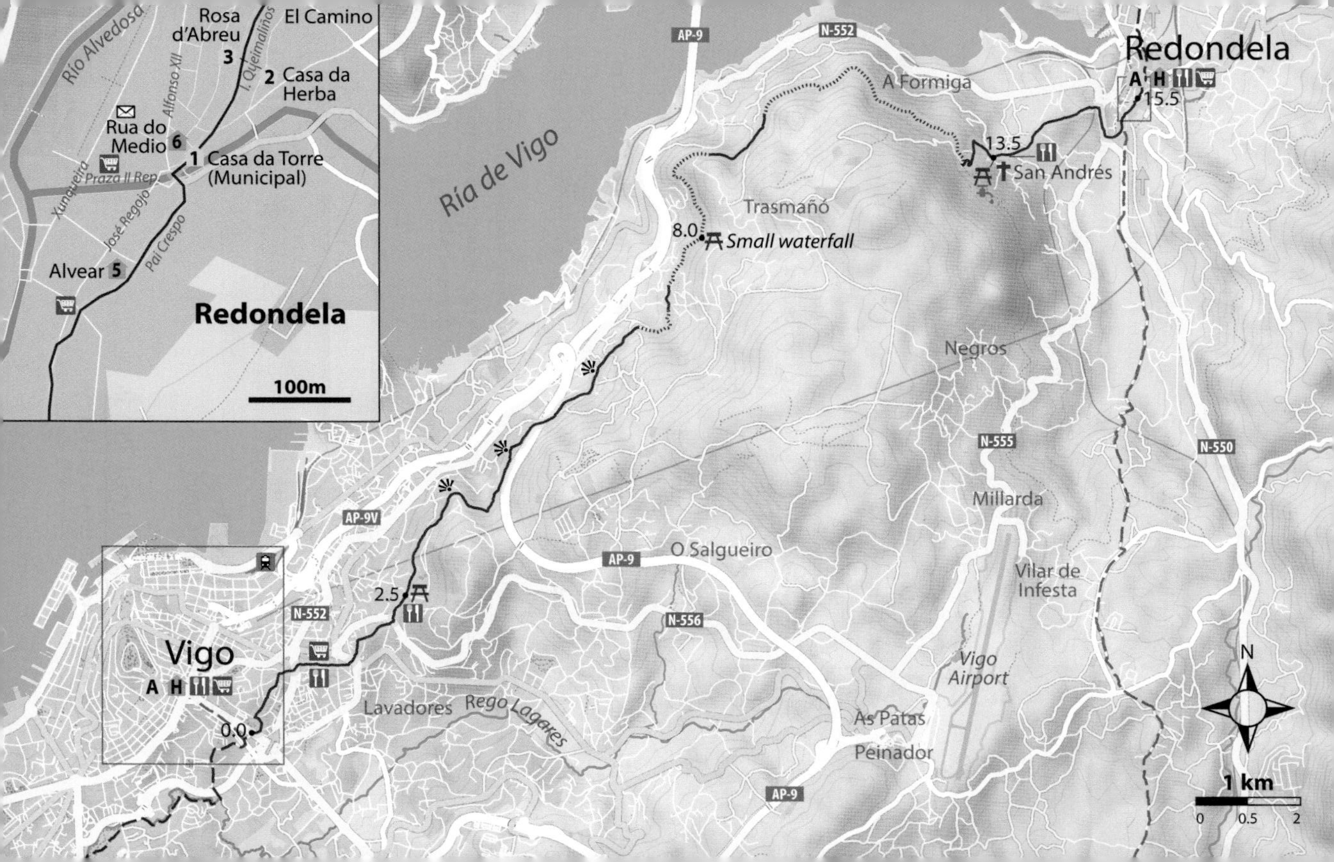
Redondela
A H
15.5
N-552
AP-9
A Formiga
13.5
San Andrés
Ría de Vigo
Trasmañó
8.0
Small waterfall
Negros
N-555
N-550
Millarda
AP-9V
O Salgueiro
AP-9
Vilar de Infesta
2.5
N-552
N-556
Vigo
A H
Vigo Airport
Lavadores
Rego Lagares
As Patas
0.0
Peinador
AP-9
N
1 km
0
0.5
2
Rosa d'Abreu
El Camino
Río Alvedosa
3
I. Queimaliños
2 Casa da Herba
Alfonso XII
Rua do Medio
6
1 Casa da Torre (Municipal)
Xunqueira
Praza II Rep.
José Regojo
Pai Crespo
Alvear 5
Redondela
100m

About the Authors

Matthew Harms is a walker and cyclist, at heart a traveler who believes in slower forms of transportation that allow for a closer understanding of people, communities, and landscapes. He has multiple years of experiences working with hiking routes in the Balkans and Middle East, and his many self-supported journeys have taken him through the Middle East, Europe, and the United States.

Anna Dintaman and **David Landis** are the cofounders of Village to Village Press, LLC and bring over 10 years of experience working with walking routes in the Mediterranean and Middle East. Both avid hikers and cyclists, their experience ranges from backpacking Patagonia and Nepal to hiking in the Alps, Andes and Appalachian mountains to cycling across the United States. They have shared a deep love of the Camino since they each separately took a 500-mile journey on the Camino Francés in 2009. In 2007, David cofounded the Jesus Trail, a hiking trail that connects sites from the life of Jesus. They enjoy introducing their children to the joys of walking, the outdoors, and learning from other cultures.

Feedback, comments & corrections welcomed: info@caminoguidebook.com

facebook.com/caminoguidebooks
instagram.com/caminoguidebook
twitter.com/caminoguidebook
pinterest.com/caminoguidebook

Village to Village Press, LLC specializes in publishing hiking guidebooks and supporting trail development projects, especially with an emphasis on pilgrimage along the Camino de Santiago and in the Middle East and Mediterranean regions.

Notes

Town & Map Index